Black Communications: Breaking Down The Barriers

Evelyn Baker Dandy, Ph.D.

AFRICAN AMERICAN IMAGES
1991
CHICAGO, ILLINOIS

5\98

#25337938

Cover illustration by Napoleon Wilkerson

ts:
all

edition, third printing

Copyright 1991 by Evelyn Baker Dandy, Ph.D.

Table of Contents

DEDICATION

This book is dedicated to Ronlyn Baker McCaskill Dandy my daughter and my friend, who first introduced me to Kunjufu's books, who has hung in there with me through thick and thin, and who is now coming into her own! God bless you and keep you, my love.

ACKNOWLEDGMENT

In the beginning was the Word, And the Word was with God, And the Word was God.

The greatest acknowledgment of gratitude for this text goes to God, who directs my paths and who enabled me to write this book as partial fulfillment of a mission.

To my husband, Jim, who served as best friend, chief advocate and financier and who endured a proliferation of books and papers as well as my preoccupation with this task. To my sons, Ronald and Russell, who have emerged as scholars in a world that offers few rewards for young Black men who strive for excellence. To my sister Ann, a master-teacher, who introduced me to books by Orlando Taylor and Mid-Atlantic Center for Race Equity.

Special acknowledgment must also be given to my friend and assistant Lisa Proffitt, who shared my commitment and expertly typed the manuscript. To Albert Greene, Beverly John, Robert Gilbert, Edward Chisholm, friends who read early drafts and offered invaluable suggestions for betterment.

To Jawanza Kunjufu, who consistently held high expectations for me and provided me the space and the opportunity to fulfill them. To Folami Prescott who consulted long-distance, presenting numerous suggestions for keeping the manuscript practical and meaningful. To Adrian Payton-Williams, who asked the right questions and offered ever so gentle nudging toward completion.

Additional acknowledgments must also be extended to the work of giants whose texts have laid the foundation for study. To Asa Hilliard, who read the chapter on African origins, quoted additional sources and reminded me of our strong literate beginnings. To Orlando Taylor, whose work has set the stage for breaking the barriers and who graciously consented to write the preface for this book. To Herman Reese, whose Infusion conferences spurred the writing of this manuscript. To the following experts: Lorenzo Dow Turner, Roger Abrahams, Robbins Burling, Ernie Smith, Geneva Smitherman Donaldson, Mary Rhodes Hoover, Rudine Sims Bishop, Shirley Lewis, Janice Hale-Benson, Shirley Brice Heath, Ivan Van Sertima, Wade Nobles, and Jawanza Kunjufu.

To my mentor, Patricia C. Nichols, a constant source of ideas and encouragement for airing concerns about my passion for the language of the children. To Otis Johnson, LaWanda Ransom, George Pinkney, Vince Edwards, and John Mangieri, friends, who inspired me with intelligent insights. To my students who asked questions, provided examples and challenged me, I am eternally grateful. To the beautiful African American children who hold our future in their hands, I respectfully acknowledge my duty to present a positive view of their language.

And, finally to my parents, Lydia Katherine and Isaiah Russell Baker, whose prayers and unwavering faith have consistently taught me to first acknowledge God and He will direct my paths.

PREFACE

On the eve of the 21st century, the United States is undergoing two significant transformations. Both have significant implications for African Americans with respect to language.

First, the United States is experiencing a radical shift in its demographic composition to include a greater percentage of people of color. According to the 1990 census, which undercounted people of color, upwards of 25% of the nation's population is comprised of African Americans, Latinos and Asian Americans. In two decades, these groups will comprise more than one-third of the nation, and about one-half by the year 2050. Each of these groups bring their norms for language and communication to what may be called the New American mosaic.

Second, the American economy is being transformed from an industrial base to a service base, and one driven by information and technology. An economy of this type must be driven by a highly literate work force which has, in turn, its own set of norms for language and communication.

It is within this context that the language behaviors and language education of African Americans must be viewed. On the one hand, African Americans like all other groups of Americans, have their own unique language and communication systems. These unique systems combine to produce the nation's rich and diverse language and communication heritage.

Yet, the language of African Americans is all too often degraded or simply dismissed by individuals from both inside and outside the racial group as being uneducated, illiterate, undignified or simply nonstandard. In this regard, the language of African Americans is unique in relation to virtually all other groups of Americans in general and groups of color in particular. Most of the other groups of color are at least given credit for having a legitimate language heritage, even if they are denied full access to American life. Who, for example, considers Spanish to be an ill-formed language, or Japanese to be an undignified language, or Chinese to be a nonstandard language? Even most of the dialects of English spoken by other Americans are considered to have value, with many being highly prized by the general public.

Many of the negative attitudes toward the language system of African Americans are based on an ignorance of the facts. Consequently, outsiders are prone to negatively stereotype African American language systems, while many African Americans themselves possess low language self-concepts.

Black Communications: Breaking Down the Barriers attempts to set the record straight with respect to African American language systems—and the culture which undergirds them. After all, a language system can never be examined completely or accurately without some attention to the culture in which it exists and the cognitive systems upon which it is based.

Black Communications: Breaking Down the Barriers correctly grounds the language system of African Americans in the proper historical and cultural perspective— in Africa! In doing so, it provides a framework for building positive attitudes and expectations with respect to African American language systems. It also provides a factual basis for African Americans to acquire more positive attitudes towards their own language.

The importance of teacher and student language attitudes cannot be overstated. They form the bases of teachers' expectations, preferred teaching strategies, school placements, many discipline problems, and referrals to special and remedial education programs.

As the United States becomes more culturally

diverse, it is imperative for African Americans to sit at the American language table as members in good and high standing, and with strong and positive self-concepts.

Now, after having argued for the beauty, legitimacy and value of traditional African American language systems, the information/technology society is such that all of its citizens must acquire the language required for citizenship and participation in it. For many groups, including African Americans, this will require the development of a kind of bilingual, bidialectal and, in some ways, a bicultural competence. In other words, African Americans, like many other groups, must acquire a language system which often differs in several significant ways from their community language systems, while preserving their community language system for use as needed.

Evelyn Dandy provides teachers with strategies that they may employ to enhance African American students' learning of the language required for academic and career success, while retaining the integrity and beauty of their home language and communication systems. Through the serious utilization of such principles, African American learners can become better poised for citizenship on the one hand and continued bonding with their indigenous community language systems on the other.

Several years ago, a noted psychologist wrote a book entitled, "My Language is Me." That's true. Perhaps more significantly, one could say, "My language is a reflection of my culture and of me." One may learn other systems of language, but one must constantly remember that his or her own system continues to be important for certain occasions and with certain people.

Through the recognition and appreciation for language and communication diversity, and the acquisition of the language of power for the information age, African Americans will be better positioned to feel good about themselves and, equally important, to become full participants in the "American Dream."

Orlando L. Taylor, Dean
School of Communications
Howard University
Washington, D.C.

INTRODUCTION

LANGUAGE AND DIALECT

From century to century, from place to place, from
situation to situation, and even from speaker to speaker,
language is forever a variable. We sometimes imagine that
English has a sort of permanence or rigidity. We suppose
that its rules are firmly codified in books of grammar, its
words all listed in dictionaries, and its pronunciations
well-specified, but if we pause for just a moment to think,
we soon realize how wrong such an idea must be. (Robbins Burling, p. 4).-

In 1973 when Burling described language, the term
"break dancing" did not exist; nor did "rap" the word that
is used for music in its current form. Words like "user
friendly," AIDS, "yo": a greeting, and "chill out" were yet
to be used in everyday conversations. Language is a
medium of exchange that people use to communicate
with one another. Language transmits our culture, it
permits us to send and to receive messages. Language
is constantly changing.

A dialect is a variation within a particular language.
All English speaking people speak a dialect of their native
language. Unfortunately, the term dialect has been used
to denote a bad style of language - something negative.
In reality, a dialect is something slightly different from
another of the same type. Even American sign language
includes a dialect variation.

A dialect is a language system identifiable to a particular region or social group. It is a variety of language generally, mutually intelligible with other varieties of that language, but set off from them by unique features of pronunciation, word order, and vocabulary. Jimmy Carter, Ted Kennedy, and Ronald Reagan all speak a dialect of their native language. Their dialects are standard for their particular region of the country.

While dialects vary regionally, they also vary across social boundaries. Now, social variation in language is often classified as standard and nonstandard. The language that is used by most educated speakers of a given region to carry out their important academic, economic, and political business is considered the standard for that region. Naturally, what is standard in one region may not be standard in another region. If the South had won the Civil War, Bryant Gumbel might speak like Lester Maddox instead of like Walter Cronkite. There is a standard English, however, that is spoken in formal situations by educated business and professional persons. This standard cuts across regional and social boundaries.

Dialects can also vary from person to person. That personal variation is called an idiolect. Every individual's idiolect develops as a result of a lifetime of experiences with language. For example, my daughter Ronlyn learned how to talk when she lived in Philadelphia. She learned the dialect of her mother, who also grew up in that area. That dialect is characterized by a strong emphasis on the letter "r". Court is pronounced /kort/; it rhymes with fort. (See Figure 1 which illustrates the relationships between language, dialects and idiolects.)

At the age of 4 1/2, Ronlyn moved with her family to Savannah, Georgia. Ronlyn started first grade with children and teachers who spoke dialects that deemphasized the r in words. In Savannah, Ronlyn heard court pronounced two different ways: court could rhyme with coat, or it could be elongated into two syllables and sound like co-wert. In an effort to fit in with the people she played with and went to school with, Ronlyn started to change her pronunciation of certain words. In fact, as she grew up, Ronlyn learned to vary her speech, depending upon her audience. Now, as an adult, she switches

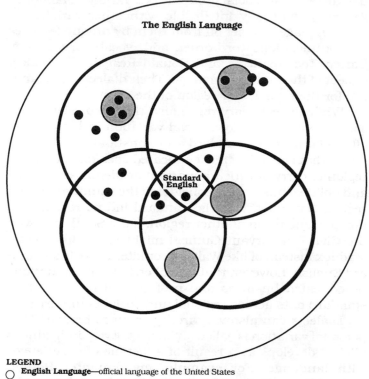

The English Language

Standard English

FIGURE 1. Language can vary on a regional, social and personal level.

her pronunciation, grammar and vocabulary to the most acceptable form depending upon the situational requirement. She has developed her own personal dialect (her idiolect). That idiolect is as much a part of Ronlyn as her own skin.

One of the school's goals for developing students' communicative competence is to have the speaker assume a variety of ways of responding, depending upon what the situation requires. There are three names for this variety: "speech registers," "speech levels," or "speech styles." Speech registers can range from formal to informal. They are speech variations appropriate to certain situations. Students should be encouraged to use a variety of registers in their speaking and in their writing.

Formal language is suited to dignified and solemn or ceremonial situations. Legal documents, scholarly journals, business reports and textbooks are generally written in formal language. The tone is serious, with advanced vocabulary and complex sentences. Informal language, also called "colloquial," is used in everyday circumstances: classroom discussions, conversations and informal talks. The tone of informal language is casual; contractions and simpler words are used. Newspaper and magazine journalists use informal language. Many professional journals are beginning to use informal language. Both formal and informal language are considered "standard language", or "standard English" (SE) or "educated English." Spoken languages are often informal. They could be subdivided into school talk, street talk, and home talk.

Slang, also called jargon, is very informal language consisting of vivid words that are most frequently used in conversation. The tone is relaxed. Words in slang are often popular but they change frequently, much the same as clothing styles. Dialect is the form of language used by speakers from a particular region of the country, social group or community. It contains features of standard language, and it may also include slang. If it appears in print, dialect is usually in the dialogue of a character or in poetry. Slang and dialect are considered nonstandard language. Here are some examples:

Standard
Formal: I shall visit Mary.
Informal: I'll go to Mary's house
Nonstandard
Slang: Uhmaw split to Mary's crib, man.
Dialect: I'm goin' to Mary house.
I'm a-goin' over Mary's house.

In 1974, the Conference on College Composition and Communication (CCCC) and the National Council of Teachers of English passed a series of resolutions affirming that students should be permitted to use their own language in the school. However, many teachers complained that they could not understand the dialect/language used by Black children. Turner (1985, p. 34) cites the background statement that has far-reaching implications for the education of African American students.

> ...When speakers of a dialect of American English claim not to be able to understand speakers of another dialect of the same language, the impediments are likely to be attitudinal. What is really the hearer's resistance to any unfamiliar form may be interpreted as the speaker's fault... When asked to respond to the content, they may be unable to do so and may accuse the speaker of being impossible to understand (Committee on CCCC Language Statement, 1974, p. 4, Turner, 1985)

The teacher's attitude toward students' language is a crucial factor in determining whether students will be active participants in the educational process. By extending their awareness of the structure of language and dialect differences, teachers can begin to improve their linguistic attitudes and subsequently develop positive expectations for those who speak different dialects. Chapter One will focus on teachers' linguistic attitudes.

CHAPTER ONE

TEACHERS' LINGUISTIC ATTITUDES

People who cannot communicate are powerless. People who know nothing of their past are culturally impoverished. People who cannot see beyond the confines of their own lives are ill-equipped to face the future. It is in the public school that this nation has chosen to pursue enlightened ends for all of its people. And this is where the battle for the future of America will be won or lost. (Ernest Boyer, 1983, p. 6)

Can Teachers Reject Dialect Renderings?

Of all the times I have observed classroom instruction, none has ever had a more lasting impact on me than the following true story. As a graduate assistant at a large Southern university, I supervised practicum students—undergraduate teacher education majors—who were having their first experiences in the classroom. What follows happened in 1981, but it is very typical of what is still going on in classrooms around the country today. As you read this vignette, put yourself in Joey's place.

A Dialect Rejection

All eight members of Joey's group were more eager than usual to go to their reading group. Today was special. Alice, the student from the University, was going to read with them. All semester, she had been working

1

individually with these third graders, helping them with handwriting and spelling, and correcting their papers. But today, she was going to "teach" the highest reading group - the best readers in the class and her supervisor was going to watch.

Joey rushed back to the table to get the seat next to Alice. He wanted to ask her if he could be the first to read.

"Have you ever felt as if nobody loved you?" asked Alice, as a means of introducing the story. Various students responded with times they had felt rejected. Lamar reported about the time he ran away from home. Tanya told of the time she got mad with her sister. Joey wiggled in anticipation.

At last, Alice called Joey to read. Confidently he began:

"Maxie. Maxie lived in three small rooms on the top floor of an old brownstone house on Orange Skreet.

"She..."

"Not skreet, Joey. Say street."

"Skreet."

"Read the sentence again."

"Maxie lived in three small rooms on the top floor of an old, brownstone house on Orange Skreet. She had lived..."

"Joey, you're not pronouncing the word correctly. I'll read it for you. 'Maxie lived in three small rooms on the top floor of an old brownstone house on Orange Street. She had lived there for many years, and every day was the same for Maxie.' Now continue, Joey."

Joey, looking puzzled, proceeded cautiously: "Every morning at exactly 7:10, Maxie's large orange cat jumped onto the middle window sill and skretched out..."

"No, Joey. You're doing it again. Say 'stretched'."

"Skretched." Joey was speaking in a muffled tone now.

"Go ahead, Joey," coaxed Alice.

But Joey could not be coaxed. He did not read any more of the story. Suddenly, he had lost his place. (Dandy, 1982, p. 22)

What do you think Joey will do the next time he is called upon to read? Joey was embarrassed in front of his peers for something he did not understand. The emphasis in this oral reading situation *should be* on reading for meaning rather than pronouncing words. Alice rejected Joey's rendition of str. She heard a different pronunciation for str and assessed that difference as "wrong." Her constant interruptions broke the flow of the story line, emphasized reading as a sounding out process, brought attention to reading word by word, and much more seriously, demoralized Joey in front of his peers. Joey was correct in reading for meaning, so he should *not* have been interrupted.

Goodman (1983) uses the term "miscue" to describe the reading of any word other than what is printed on the page. Sims (1972) discussed the concept of miscue quality. A miscue that does not cause a loss of information or interfere with the originally intended meaning of the passage is high quality, meaning this miscue is closely related to the actual word in print. Johnson (1975, p. 535) calls Joey's alternation of skr for str during oral reading a "dialect shift" - a translation without a loss in comprehension. According to Johnson, a dialect shift occurs whenever the reader's response is:

1. Different from what actually appears in print - Joey said skreet instead of street and skretch instead of stretch;

2. Consistent with the sounds, meaning and word order features of the dialect - skr for str is a phonological (sound) feature of Black Communications; and

3. Does not result in a loss of comprehension - the printed message remains the same - Joey's translation was a direct one. He did not change the meaning of the sentence.

(See Chapter Seven for a more in-depth discussion of dialect shifts and their application to the reading process.)

Joey's dialect rejection prompted me to conduct some research on this phonological feature. (See Dandy, 1988.) Labov (1970) maintains that this alternate pronunciation was an extreme tendency "...common enough among Negro speakers in South Carolina". Burling (1973) classifies skreet for street as an example of word variability - a special pronunciation given to a few random words. Wolfram and Fasold (1974) contend that this "nonstandard pronunciation" is found in the speech of younger children and given up automatically as children grow older. I had heard the same pronunciation in adults and children (many of whom were required to attend speech correction classes) in Pennsylvania as well as

3

Georgia and South Carolina. Since this study, I have heard the str alternation in Nashville, Tennessee and as far away as Elkhart, Indiana.

A study of 228 nine- and ten-year-old students from three schools in Georgia and South Carolina reveals that skr for str is indeed a dialectal rendition, for it was used by approximately one-third of the Black children in all three schools. No White children used the alternation.

There is evidence that skr for str comes from the Gullah dialect, spoken in the coastal areas of Georgia and South Carolina by African Americans who are direct descendants from Gambia, Liberia, Nigeria, Mozambique, Angola, and other countries in Africa. This excerpt from *De Gullah Storybook (1989)*, by Daise, contains the skr alternation. Ron Daise (personal communication) reports that the alternation is common in Gullah speakers.

"De Gullah gone a saachin een de maash fa git some grass fa weave een ta some bask ut, bot six gayta dar um fa pass! De lay screch out ee de wata en won leh um go him way."

Translation:

"The Gullah went searching in the marsh to get some grass to weave into some baskets, but six alligators dared him to pass! They lay stretched out in the water and wouldn't let him go his way." (p. 14)

Skr for str is a feature of Black Communications. Alice believed that Joey had a speech problem and was not pronouncing the word correctly. But Joey was reading for meaning. He was switching the *visual code* he read to the *verbal code* he uses. Asking Joey to instantly rearrange his phonemic inventory and produce a sound he does not habitually use for the symbols str would be like asking a Southern dialect speaker to say /pen/ instead of /pin/ in "Pick up your pen and write the word,"; or asking a Hispanic-American dialect speaker to say /shoos/ instead of /choos/ in "I want to buy some shoes"; or asking a Bostonian dialect speaker to say /car/ instead of /cah/ in "The car is in the garage." Your dialect is just as much a part of you as your own skin!

4

Should Teachers Allow Dialects in the Classroom?

Let's go back to Alice. Her inaccurate assessment of Joey's dialect shift is common for many White and Black preservice and in-service teachers all over the country. Any construction that differs from that used by the teacher is usually interpreted as wrong or bad.

Twenty years ago, when the children in my classes in Philadelphia used <u>skreet</u> for <u>street</u> and other constructions such as "She at her mamma house" and "there it go" (to refer to the location of a paper in a box), I made a similar interpretation. Hearing those constructions was like listening to sharp fingernails scrape across a chalkboard. I had been trained by my parents, by my teachers and by the undergraduate teacher education faculty that "that kind of talk" had no place in the school. So, whenever the children I taught used it, I would correct them by saying it the other way and having the students repeat after me. I would not allow "that kind of talk" in my classroom. My training had led me to believe the dialect was inferior.

Disallowing dialect renderings can have a negative effect on classroom interaction because it reduces the spontaneity of a student's responses. Exciting circumstances, those heavily laden with emotion, often trigger the use of a more familiar comfortable way of talking. Of course, standard English must be taught, for it is the accepted language of the dominant culture of the United States and it is expected in political and economic arenas. However, if children are corrected every time they open their mouths, they will become extremely self-conscious and reluctant to speak. Teachers need to *listen* to dialect renderings so that they can understand what the children are doing with the language. Corrections in oral readings need only be made when the miscue does not fit into the context of the sentence, when it changes the meaning in some way. Emphasis should always be placed on meaning in oral reading. Oral reading should never be conducted round robin style with one child reading after another and all other children watching the text. However, like Alice, most teachers are unaware of which constructions they should correct. They cannot differentiate between a miscue and a dialect shift. (See the activities in Chapter Four for more information on miscues.)

What Does Research Say About Language Awareness?

Cunningham (1976) confirmed lack of knowledge about dialects in a study she conducted of teachers' correction responses to Black dialect miscues which did not change meanings. Teachers responded as Alice did. Cunningham observed that 189 teachers from four geographic regions corrected 78% of the dialect - specific translations, considering them as errors. Her conclusion was:

> Teachers need to be adequately trained to understand the dialects of the children they teach, and especially, to recognize meaning equivalence. In addition to this understanding, teachers must learn the acceptance of Black dialect as a complex grammatical system... It is the responsibility of teacher-training institutions to see to it that they [teachers] are taught. (p. 652)

However, Shuy (1975) reports that college curricula offer virtually no preparation for dealing with "minority" language issues. Teachers teach from their own cultural traditions (Nichols, 1990). Teacher trainees are rarely exposed to African American faculty and are given very few opportunities to interact with children of other cultures. According to their recent interviews with educators, Nelson-Barber and Meier (1990) conclude that there is still a pervasive assumption that poor, "minority" students do not do well in school. Yet, Edmonds (1979, 1981) conducted extensive research that ushered in the entire effective schools movement when he and others located schools around the country that were instructionally effective for "minority" (inner-city) children. (See Brookover and Lezotte, 1979; Brookover et.al 1982; Madden, Lawson, and Sweet, 1976; Weber, 1971; and Phi Delta Kappa, 1980.) These effective researchers found ample evidence that, in spite of the family background of the student, schools can make a difference in the lives of poor, "minority," and inner-city children.

Students' ability to use the linguistic table manners their teachers expect is a key element in determining not only teachers' attitudes, but their assessments of students' potential as learners (Gere and Smith, p. 26). There is ample evidence that teachers communicate their beliefs in students' potential through their classroom behaviors. Expectations affect the way teachers behave, and the way teachers behave affects the ways children respond. Low expectations become a self-fulfilling prophecy. In fact, Good and Brophy (1987, pp. 128-129) cite more than eighty references that confirm teachers' differential treatment for those they perceive as low achievers. Teachers interrupt these children more frequently in their oral reading, call on them less frequently, give them less time to answer questions, provide less verbal and nonverbal feedback for their answers, and provide them with less eye contact and positive nonverbal attention.

Nelson-Barber and Meier (1990) address teachers' attitudes about linguistic ability:

> Much has been made of poor and minority children's lack of verbal responsiveness in the classroom. Yet a growing body of ethno-graphic research suggests that often what these children have to say may simply be out of sync with what the teacher is asking or with the way she is asking, either because the teacher lacks the relevant cultural knowledge to elicit students' participation, or because her interactive style is unfamiliar to students. (p.3)]

Pine and Hilliard (1990) contend that a current sense of urgency is needed in school reform as the pool of candidates for teaching positions becomes increasingly White and as conscious and unconscious expressions of racism still persist in the schools. Taylor (1987) confirms that cross-cultural communication is an essential dimension of effective education.

> Students with different cultural norms are at-risk if teachers have little knowledge, sensitivity or appreciation of the diversity of communication styles. Such teachers may respond to students' diversity with negative attitudes, lowered expectations, culturally inappropriate teaching and assessment procedures, and perceptions of differences as problems. (p.1)

Alice thought Joey's different pronunciation was a problem, just as many teachers from the three schools I surveyed referred children to speech class because they made the skr/str alternation. But, it was their dialect, not a speech impediment.

Smith (1974) and Foster (1986) describe teachers' reactions to language as a "persistent dilemma" in the schools and complain that undergraduate, graduate, and in-service education courses do not prepare teachers to teach underprepared minority students. Hill (1989) confirms that teachers who enter the profession in the 1990's and beyond will simply have to teach minority students because demographic trends predict that their numbers are growing daily. Blacks and Hispanics are no longer "minorities" in California, Texas, and Florida.

How Can Teachers Broaden Linguistic Perspectives?

Labov (1970) studied reading problems of inner-city Black youth and found a yearly decline in the reading performance. He attributed the reading failure to a cultural conflict between the students and the teacher - a miscommunication. The difficulty, posited Labov, was in the fact that neither player knew how to communicate with the other. Taylor (1987) and Kochman (1981) describe discourse rules that exist among cultural groups and say that speakers follow certain assumptions within their respective cultures when they interact with those from different cultures. Miscommunication can occur when teachers fail to understand language and culture and label students with pejorative terms such as "deprived," "disadvantaged," and "nonverbal."

Shuy (1975) surveyed teachers' attitudes about the language of "disadvantaged" children and found "gross overgeneralizations," "imprecise descriptions," and a "large scale of ignorance" from teachers in their attempt to describe the problems:

1. Teachers equated lack of school vocabulary with an overall lack of vocabulary. If the children did not talk much at school and were unfamiliar with the school related terms, teachers inferred that children just didn't have a vocabulary.

2. Teachers characterized children's grammar by saying they did not speak in sentences or complete thoughts and that they used strange grammatical constructions.

3. Teachers complained that the children did not use

8

their tongue, teeth and lips and that they mispronounce words because they did not know the "correct" sounds. (pgs. 170-171)

Shuy proposes content courses for helping teachers to solve language differences/problems in their classrooms. He suggests that teachers need to *understand* language variation - why it varies and the attitudes of subgroups toward it. Teachers should be trained to *listen* to the language of their students and learn how systematic various dialects can be, so that they can develop sensitivity toward communicating with the language/dialect different child. Good and Brophy (1987) suggest that empirical studies should be conducted in classrooms in naturalistic settings. A new "thought-set" on the part of the teachers is essential. Heath (1983) reported on successful efforts to change that thought-set by having teachers build bridges between school and home by fostering increased communication. Gere and Smith (1979) contend that attitudinal change takes a conscious effort which entails the modification of one's thinking. They outline five essential steps in the change process:

1. Awareness of language development and its role in educating children;
2. Interest in terms of internal and external forces that gives impetus for change;
3. Evaluation by change agents who can provide alternate strategies and resources;
4. Trial of new approaches with opportunities for peer feedback; and
5. Adoption/Adaptation with the development of a linguistic support group to empower teachers to change linguistic perspectives.

Banks (1988) suggests that teacher preparation programs must provide diverse experiences such as seminars, visitations in real classrooms, multimedia materials, and cross-cultural interactions - all of which must be specifically designed to address attitudes. Taylor (1987) offers a cultural perspective approach to teaching standard language that does not blame the victim and devalue or seek to eliminate the learner's dialect, but uses it as an instructional base much the same as English is used to teach a foreign language. Stanford University will be moving in the right direction beginning Fall, 1991. All undergraduates will be required to take cultural diversity classes (*Jet*, Jan 7, 1991, p. 10). Along the same lines, the state of Oklahoma has passed legislation requiring teacher educators to take courses in multicultural education.

All of these points must be kept in mind as teachers seek to communicate with their students and broaden their own linguistic perspectives. The overwhelming concern in current literature is not that the dialect causes problems in reading, but that *teachers' responses* to the dialect reflect low expectations about the abilities of those who use it in the classroom, setting up barriers between teachers and students. Expectations become self-fulfilling prophecies. Teachers' perceptions do shape students' performance. However, teacher preparation programs fail to acquaint them with specific cultural and dialectal differences. In order to effectively communicate with their students, teachers must alter their linguistic perspectives.

Children are our future. The teaching-learning process requires two-way communication between teacher and student. Through their interactions, teachers prepare children to become productive citizens: to listen, to read, to speak, and to write effectively. Indeed, teachers have the power to shape the future, if they communicate with their students, but those who cannot communicate are powerless.

According to Gere and Smith (1979), step one is *awareness*. Teachers must first become aware that everyone speaks a dialect and that a dialect rendering does, in fact, communicate. Joey knew the meaning of street and stretch. Alice's *attitude* and her subsequent rejection of Joey's dialect shift caused the problem for Joey. Her naivete' about the language/dialect prohibited her from making the appropriate response.

CHAPTER TWO

BLACK COMMUNICATIONS

Black Americans have always been considered second-class citizens in a class-conscious society.... As Blacks began to redefine themselves as "beautiful people" with a proud, noble heritage, the attention of the dominant culture turned to the question of intelligence. The vehicle was the fact that Blacks were failing to read and write in public schools, despite the various programs designed to help them to do so. Some theorized genetic inferiority, while others postulated that Blacks speak a degenerate form of English which prevented their learning of standard English. (Albert Greene, 1981, p. 1)

A System of Speaking Behaviors

In this book, I want to focus on a dialect that has been labeled by a large segment of the population as nonstandard. Many names for this dialect/language exist. Some call it Black English. Other names include Vernacular Black English, Nonstandard English, Black Dialect, Ebonics (from ebony and phonetics), Negro Nonstandard English, Black Language, Inner-City English, Black Street Speech and just simply Dialect. The majority of those terms are negative, reflecting what society has conditioned people to think of them. Hoover (1985) suggests the term Black Communications (BC) because she says that the dialect is more than just speech.

11

According to Hoover and Abrahams, Black Communications includes:

1. A speech code with sounds, such as "axe" for "ask"; words such as "bad" meaning "good"; intonation such as "mmh hmm" pronounced slowly and with a low pitch to mean "I told you so"; word meanings, and grammar;

2. Speech acts or verbal strategies such as testifying, sounding, marking, signifying, and rapping, which initially was used as a language for power exchange and also included talk from a Black man to a Black woman for the purpose of winning her emotional and sexual affections;

3. Style that includes call and response, improvisation, and dramatic repetition such as "I have a dream that ..." in Martin Luther King's speech, Jesse Jackson's 1984 speech for the Democratic Convention, and Aretha Franklin's soulful tunes;

4. Nonverbal behavior such as silence and response to a ridiculous question, kinetics, or side-by-side stance in conversation, and oculesics or eye rolling to indicate disgust or resentment;

5. Sociolinguistic rules for speaking such as avoidance of the use of "boy" for man, "gal" in reference to maid, or the term "you people" to refer to Blacks;

6. Special speaking behaviors such as personal Black talk used by Blacks who are familiar with and trust one another. (Abrahams, 1972) - Subjects include "We still got a long way to go", and "ain't White folks crazy";

7. Moral teachings through proverbs and other wise sayings such as "What goes around comes around" and "a chip off the old block don't fly far."

Black Communications is a system of speaking behavior. The language is alive and well and is spoken everywhere African Americans reside in America.

For years though, African Americans have been admonished to hide their language:

Since the beginning of their heritage in this country as slaves, Blacks have been dominated and victimized by a culture determined to show and maintain its superiority physically, culturally and intellectually. The notion first manifested itself when Blacks were shackled and subjected to all types of abuse. When the slaves were granted freedom, ending physical bondage, their cultural values

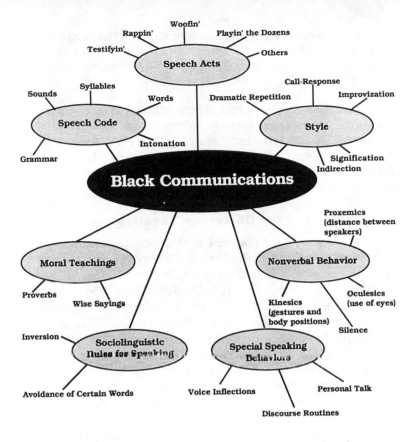

FIGURE 2. Black Communications is not just a speech code.
It is a system of communication.

were then challenged and condemned, they were called uncouth and violent; they were ugly with thick lips and kinky hair; and they were incapable of achieving anything worthwhile. (Greene, 1981, p. 1)

Even today, this dialect is regarded by Whites as well as some Blacks as very negative. It is described as "broken", "flat," "ghetto," "country," "bad," "unsuitable for school," and "unsuitable for the work place," and Blacks who use the dialect are considered unintelligible and ignorant.

The Deficit and the Difference Theories

This "nonverbal" concept that describes Black Communications is called the Deficit Theory. Those who use the dialect have a deficit - something is missing in their language system; it is not fully developed. This theory was adopted for "culturally disadvantaged children" in the 1960s. One response to the thinking that Blacks had a language deficiency was manifested in highly-structured educational programs such as DISTAR (Direct Instruction Systems for Teaching Arithmetic and Reading), developed by Science Research Associates in 1968. Teachers were required to follow a rigid step-by-step approach for preschool children so that when they learned to speak they could join their "privileged" classmates in kindergarten and first grade.

Another theory about the dialect arose in the 1970s as a result of the work done by Labov (1975) who conducted in-depth studies of inner-city children in Philadelphia. He concluded that Nonstandard English is just as logical and consistent as Standard English. Nonstandard English could be reproduced, and it makes sense. It is merely different. Hence, the Difference Theory.

Geneva Smitherman (1977) discusses the Difference and Deficit Theories in her text, *Talkin' and Testifyin.'* She agrees that the Deficit Theory is erroneous, but the Difference Theory is no better because, in American society, anything that is different from the mainstream is considered deficient or bad anyway. Smitherman contends that many African Americans abandoned their dialect (and their culture) and adopted the culture of

14

mainstream society thinking they would be given automatic acceptance into that culture. According to Smitherman, some 80 to 90 percent of African Americans speak the dialect at one time or another. According to most African American audiences I address, 95 percent *understand* the dialect. The remaining 5 percent may not be telling the truth, or they may have never been exposed to those who use the dialect.

Alexander (1985) contends that there are even variations within the dialect spoken by African Americans. The variety used is determined by a person's sex, age, socioeconomic status, geographical area in which she spent her formative years, the speaker's purpose, the setting, the topic, and the audience.

Three Points about the System

While there is disagreement about what this dialect is called and how it is perceived, there is agreement among researchers and linguists on three very important points. I want you to remember these, if you do not remember anything else about or any dialect or language system, for that matter:

1. Not all Blacks speak this dialect all of the time. Many Blacks are bidialectal. They engage in code switching and code shifting much like Ronlyn, my daughter, using her own personal dialect as she uses different sounds and words depending upon her audience.

2. Black Communications shares many features with other dialects of English. You will hear several similarities between BC and Appalachian English spoken by those who live in the Appalachian Mountains.

3. Black Communications is rule governed. This is a legitimate linguistic system that has rules. Labov (1970) wrote several treaties on "The Study of Nonstandard English."

These three facts about dialect will be addressed in subsequent chapters. They are confirmed by the following: Sledd (1965), Labov (1970), Maxwell (1970), Burling (1973), Smith (1974), Wolfram and Fasold (1974), Stoller (1975), Pearson (1977), Smitherman (1977), Yellin (1980), Alexander (1985), Scott (1985), Stice (1987), and Dandy (1988 and 1991). (See the References for a complete listing of these sources.)

The optimum attitude to adopt about dialects and languages is well stated by Wolfram and Fasold (1974, p. 15) it is "...a basic respect for the linguistic worth of all languages and dialects as linguistic codes." Black Communications has many features: a speech code, speech acts, style, nonverbal behaviors, sociolinguistic rules, special speaking behaviors, and moral teachings. All are legitimate channels of communication.

As I travel throughout the United States and speak to audiences of all races, I receive confirmation on the many features. People of all races have commented that they hear others use the features. They give corroboration to the importance of communication in the classroom. Language is the medium of instruction. It is used for assessment, interpersonal relationships, group interactions, and counseling. The way we interact and react comes from our culture. Culture shapes the way we perceive, organize, process, and use information. Indeed, the way we communicate emanates from our culture.

CHAPTER THREE

AFRICAN ORIGINS

Africans in the African diaspora, including the Americans and the Caribbeans retained and still retain varying degrees of African culture. That culture is reflected in family patterns, language, religious belief systems, artistic creativities, etc. (Asa Hilliard, 1985, p.155)

Culture is defined as the values, symbols, interpretations and perspectives that distinguish one group of people from another (Banks, 1989). People who are a part of the same culture usually interpret the meanings of symbols, artifacts and behaviors in the same or at least similar ways. Culture is transmitted within the group through expressive means: language, music, dance, and even food; specifically, its preference, preparation and manner of consumption (Dodson and Ross, 1977).

We are a product of our culture. We interpret our world through our culture. Culture shapes the way we think, the way we learn, the way we talk. Culture serves to unite us as a group. It determines our customs and even the way we interact with one another.

Never before did I realize the impact of the African American culture as when I moved from Philadelphia to Savannah. Initially, I was overwhelmed by the stark contrasts between the cultural traditions in the North and in the South, but as I began to participate in

17

community activities, I found numerous similarities. Now, as I read and watch and listen to Black Communications spoken around the world, I realize that many of our cultural traditions have a common thread. These traditions are similar across the diaspora - wherever Africans have settled. Many of them have been preserved in the language, particularly in the emphasis placed on words and the ways they are used.

There are Black Americans who take offense when they hear of connections being made between their cultural traditions and those of Africa. Some Blacks have made every effort to disassociate themselves from anything remotely related to Africa. To some, assimilation into the dominant culture entails this kind of detachment from "Blackness."

Historically, Africa has been viewed as a "country" filled with deep, dark jungles and savages - an image largely created in the movie "Tarzan, the Apeman." Woodson's *Miseducation of the Negro* (1933) documented efforts to denigrate Africans and their culture:

> You might study the history as it was offered in our system from the elementary school throughout the university, and you would never hear Africa mentioned except in the negative. You would thereby learn that Africans first never domesticated the sheep, goat, cow, developed the idea of trial by jury, produced the first stringed instruments, and gave the world its greatest boon in the discovery of iron. (Carter G. Woodson, 1933, p. 21)

More recently, Africa has been portrayed as the continent where AIDS may have originated, a land of famine and starvation for millions of children, the seat of unrest and Apartheid. Negative terms related to Africa and Blackness abound. In 1973, Ossie Davis studied Roget's *Thesaurus of the English Language* and found 120 synonyms for the word "Blackness". Davis categorized 60 of those words as "...distinctly unfavorable and none of them as mildly positive" (p. 73).

Great "things" have come out of Africa, and although many of the contributions provided by our native land have been lost, hidden or stolen (James, 1954), there has been a resurgence of interest in African materials and documentation of contributions made by Africa to the history of the world.

A Strong Literate Beginning

There is ample evidence that the language of Africa began with a strong literate tradition. The Bushmen of Southern Africa wrote in stone about their daily activities. Egyptian mythology recorded on papyrus the deeds of ancient ancestors. Inscriptions on sacred texts, monuments, carvings, paintings, pottery, and European classical writing provided evidence that Kemetic (Egyptian) education was a model for early European education in Greece and Rome (Hilliard, 1985, pp. 153-155). Writing among priests and royalty had been prominent, according to Asante (1987). Negative myths about Africa have recently been dispelled.

Africa is the second largest continent. According to Richard Leaky (February 4, 1991 lecture, Savannah, GA), Africa is four times larger than the United States. Only ten percent of the continent is covered by jungle, less than the amount found in the country of Brazil. This continent holds the world's largest mineral deposits: gold, diamond, uranium, and chromium. Historians and researchers such as Cheikh Anta Diop, John Henrik Clarke, Ivan Van Sertima, Martin Bernal, Asa Hilliard, and others have documented numerous contributions made by Africans to the world prior to the 2,000 years of penetration by European invaders, who ravaged the land. Here are some of those facts that have been recorded:

1. Mankind started in Africa (Diop, 1986, p.167; Clark, 1972, p. xi; Hilliard, 1985, p. 155; Bernal, 1987, pp. 11-12).

2. From 700-1800 A.D. during West Africa's Golden Age the empires of Songhay, Mali, Ghana, and Kamen-Bornu were trade and cultural centers (Harris, 1990, pp. LA 9-23).

3. Greek philosophy originated in Egypt where Greek philosophers studied (James, 1954, pp. 130, 183-184; Bernal, 1984, pp. 11-12).

4. In 4236 BC, Egyptians invented the calendar and as early as the fourth millennium B.C. they had created the leap year (Diop, 1986, p. 78).

19

5. The alphabet was invented by Africans (Van Sertima, 1989, pp. 24-25).

Because of the prohibitions on teaching enslaved Africans to read and write, many of the cultural traditions and contributions of Africa have been preserved in the language of African Americans, especially with its emphasis on the oral tradition - in verbal as well as nonverbal communication. The culture has been preserved in the oral language - the music, stories, folk sayings, jokes, food, and most especially in the ways words are used.

The Oral Tradition

Linguistic scholars have studied languages and dialects in an effort to determine their origins. Since none of the scholars were alive when the languages evolved, they cannot say with certainty what happened. However, they have cited evidence to support their views.

Black Communications, as it exists today, probably developed through a sort of leveling process as a result of cultural contact and interaction: 1) cultural transmission among the enslaved Africans who, before they came to America, devised bridge-languages to communicate among various tribes; and 2) contact among language different speakers from communities throughout Africa- some of whom were deposited in the West Indies and later brought to this country and European slave traders and settlers from Portugal, Holland, France and England, who colonized parts of Africa, South America, the West Indies, and the New World.

The Black communication system described in Chapter Two has its roots in the indigenous languages of Africa. According to Van Sertima, a linguist and anthropologist, nearly all of the languages of Africa came from three main families: the Sudanic, the Bantu, and the Hamitic. (Welmers (1973) lists four: Afro-Asiatic, Nilo-Saharan, Niger-Kordo-fanian and Khoisan.) Van Sertima reports that New World slaves came from Sudanic and the Bantu which included such languages as Twi, Ewe, Yoruba, Wolof, Temne, Mende, Mandingo, Ibo, Nupe, Efik, Mossi, Jukun, and Kanuri. Vass (1979, p. 11), who spent 40 years in Africa and studied the languages and slave trade routes, contends that the majority of enslaved Africans brought to the New World came from Angola and Mozambique. According to Vass, Bantu speech had its original nucleus in Nigeria, spread southward into central Africa and encompassed languages such as Kongo, Lwena, Luba-Kasai, Luba-katanga, Bemba, Ila, Rundi, Swahili, Nyanja, Yao, and others (p.3). Indeed, Van Sertima (1971, pp. 15-20), Mbiti (1990, p. 99), an African scholar, and Vass (1979, p.3) agree that there were enough similarities among the tribal languages to enable them to communicate among themselves. The major characteristic of the broad group of Bantu languages was its ability to "...move into a culture to absorb it, and to change its language" (Vass, p.3). There were also similarities in the rhythms, gestures, and movements created by the Africans. Africans possessed what Taylor calls "mythaphonics", a combination of speech, music, dance, and nonverbal communication which they brought to the new land.

Vass (1979, pp. 9-19) reports that between the early 1700s and mid-to late-1800s, some 9,566,000 Africans were imported to South America, the Caribbean Islands, the United States, Central America, Mexico, and Canada. This number does not reflect the lives lost during the Middle Passage, nor those Africans imported illegally after the ban on slave importation. Since the U.S. government imposed heavy taxes on slaves imported from the Caribbean and places other than Africa, after traders depleted the supply of those enslaved from West Africa, they developed sophisticated trade routes reaching far into Central and Eastern Africa to gather tribes of "new" Negroes to bring to this country. In many locations in the New World, enslaved Africans outnumbered Whites - especially in the state of South Carolina, where large numbers were imported directly from West Africa and Angola in Central Africa.

When the Portuguese came to Africa to trade, the Africans took the words of the Europeans and fit these words into their own sounds and word order systems and devised trade languages or pidgins. By the end of the 1700s, Black communication systems were established along the coast of West Africa. Van Sertima terms them Black Portuguese, Black French, Black Dutch, and Black English.

Black Communications were carried here in the hearts and minds of enslaved Africans who, some 9 1/2 million strong, were brought by force to a hostile land. Only the most able-bodied were stolen from their homeland and only the strongest and most determined survived the Middle Passage between Africa and the New World. Reports of uprisings on the slave ships confirmed the Africans' dissatisfaction with this new condition and their efforts to unite, regardless of tribal affiliation. It may well have occurred the way Alex Haley portrayed life in the epic, *Roots.* Remember the scene during which the Mandingo warrior encouraged the Africans to plan ways to overthrow the Europeans on the slave ship. His words to Kunta Kinte (in Roots, Volume 1, Warner Home Video) were "Men chained together are brothers. We are all one village." The bridge languages begun among the African tribes were revived in the Middle Passage (Van Sertima, 1971, p. 19).

Those who survived the "middle passage" arrived chained and malnourished in a different land. They brought with them no books, no luggage, no mementos - only the clothes they had on their backs. Although the plantation system discouraged communication among the slaves under penalty of death, these New World Africans still maintained conversations with one another in an effort to strengthen in-group solidarity and plan revolt (Dalby, p. 173).

In America, the nature of social relationships isolated New World Africans from the rest of society. This isolation enabled the slaves to maintain their culture in spite of the separation from their homeland. As new shipments arrived, the older enslaved Africans were charged with teaching them how to live on the plantation. These shipments probably provided the way to continually perpetuate African idiom and customs as "new" slaves intermingled with "old" ones.

The enslaved Africans devised covert ways of communicating and disguised messages in their words, their songs, and their behaviors. The Underground Railroad, a system designed to help slaves escape to free states and Canada, had its own set of codes. Alleyne (1980, p.

17) tells of African secret ritual languages that remained intact and were used in religious practices. Walker (1987) describes the hidden meanings of escape to freedom in slave songs and spirituals. Guffy (in Foster, 1986) has recorded historical accounts of a secret game played by slaves that taught them how to control themselves in the face of verbal and physical insults from their masters. Dalby (1972, p. 172) speaks of efforts to "... deceive, confuse, and conceal information from White people in general." Holt (1972) describes a language code that facilitated in-group communication. Burley (in Foster, 1986) describes insults hurled by field slaves at house slaves to vent their anger and ways they kept the master from catching them as they taunted the "more favored" house slaves. African connections to this game are documented by Smitherman (1977), Nobles (1980), and Foster (1986), who report on similar African initiation rites: Ashanti opo verses, Trinidadian games, and Caribbean performances - all related to special ways of using language.

Modern counterparts to this kind of talk are described by Abrahams (1976) who defines a hidden in-group language that changes to maintain the hidden quality. This hidden group language evolved into "street talk" that used verbal strategies such as rappin', woofin', and playin' the dozens. (See Chapter Five on verbal strategies.)

When two speakers of different languages make an effort to communicate, they use only the most essential words and place them in the fundamental structure to which they are accustomed. Although the slaves were forced to learn new words in order to respond to their European captors, they retained the basic structure and idiom of their native language. As they communicated with their captors, a language of contact derived. This "convenient" language is called a *pidgin*. There is evidence that pidgins, as language variations, existed on the shores of West Africa (Dillard, 1973).

Pidgins can become native languages when the children of pidgin speakers are cut off from the languages spoken by their parents. The new language that evolves is called a *creole*. Gullah or Geechee is considered a creole. It is spoken today by African Americans who live in coastal South Carolina and Georgia also adjacent areas of North Carolina and Florida and are direct descendants of Gambia, Liberia, Nigeria, Sierre Leone, Angola, and other countries of Africa. To this day, the Gullah language has remained intact, largely because of the isolation of its speakers and their efforts to maintain cultural solidarity. In fact, Mille (1990) has found ample evidence to support the concept that Gullah has remained virtually the same over the past 130 years.

Connections have been made between the West African languages and Gullah, between Gullah and Black Communications and between Black Communications and other dialects of American English. According to Herskovits (1941), there seems to be a continuum that represents Africanisms in the New World cultures. The scale begins with African languages and extends to creoles in the Caribbean and in South America. It goes on to creoles such as Gullah, then to the language of rural and urban speakers of Jamaica to working class Blacks in America and to middle class African Americans and finally to mainstream European-Americans in the dominant culture. Both ends of the continuum - African languages and European languages - have affected one another (Alleyne, pp. 18-21).

Afrika (1990) describes a Gullah language path that resulted from a common linguistic connection motivated by Europeans who sought African technology and labor to build America.

> The cargo ships loaded with slaves and cargo would start in European countries, such as Ireland, England, France, Spain, Italy, and Portugal, then go to Africa, the Canary Islands, Cape Verde across the Atlantic Ocean then to South America, Haiti, Barbados, Hispaniola and Cuba. Then on to the Gulf of Mexico which includes Louisiana and Alabama, then to the Bahamas and then the Gullah slave-concentrated areas of the Sea Islands (Florida, Georgia, South and North Carolina) and then Bermuda, p.3.

Lorenzo Dow Turner (1949) a scholar of West African languages, studied Gullah for 15 years and found 4,000 Africanisms used in Gullah. Dalby (1972, pp. 172-186) lists the following terms that have come from African languages: *yam, okra, banana, tote* (meaning carry), *cola* as in Coca-Cola, *bad, poor joe, day-clean, done, hear, man, okay, uh-huh* (meaning yes), *uh-uh,* no, and *you-all* - all of which have been traced to West African languages such as Wolof, Mandingo, Akan, and Hausa.

J. Mason Brewer, a collector of American folklore, maintains that the folk literature of the American Negro has a rich African background. (See Smitherman, 1977, p. 101.) Sithole (1972, pp. 73-74) a native Zulu, found much similarity between the work songs, dance songs, and spirituals in Africa and those of Black America. He points out that the scales used in songs such as "Swing Low, Sweet Chariot" and the art of improvisation can be traced to African origins. In music, the emphasis is on rhythm rather than melody. It is likely that because Africans were forbidden by law to read and write, oral expression or word of mouth became the primary mode for maintaining the culture. Janice Hale-Benson (1986) lists the following aspects of Black culture that reflect Africanisms:

1. funerals
2. folklore (Uncle Remus stories)
3. song and dance
4. ways of dressing hair
5. wearing of scarves
6. etiquette such as titles for older people
7. child-naming practices
8. conception of the devil and religious and spiritual expressive styles
9. magical practices
10. motor habits such as walking, postures, burden carrying
11. concept of time
12. cooperation and sharing
13. audience and performance styles (pp. 16-17)

In answer to the question "What Has Africa Given America?" Herskovits (1966) lists such contributions as the musical quality of Southern language, politeness of speech, and proper behaviors that include good manners, respect for elders, and an emphasis on etiquette. He describes the ultimate effect African languages have had upon the Southern dialect:

> What happened, then, when Negroes came to the New World? They learned new words-in English, Spanish, Portuguese or French-but they spoke these words with a West African pronunciation and poured their new vocabulary into the mode of West African grammatical and idiomatic forms. And, having done this, many of them were entrusted with raising the children of their masters. From whom, then, did these White children learn to speak? Obviously from their Negro nurses, as many Southerners acknowledge. (p. 171)

Although there is ample evidence to suggest that pre-slavery Africa was both oral and literate (Hilliard, 1990 personal communication) most of the elements of African culture brought to America were carried in the oral tradition by word of mouth. They evolved as a result of the culture, the environment and the needs of the people. The oral tradition, then, became the purveyor of African culture (Smith, 1974, p. 91). Deeply embedded in the culture were their guidelines for living and an Africentric view of the world.

Language and the African World View

The African world view emphasized religion as a way of life, a strong kinship system, a symbolic concept of time, and the magic power of the word. These concepts evolved into the deep structure or the underlying meanings in the language as it is used today by Africans across the diaspora.

Religion Permeated Life

Essential to their world view was the belief in God as the creator and sustainer of all things. According to Tarynor (1976), an African clergyman, God officiated over the spiritual world and the material world. Mbiti describes the importance of religion to the African world view:

> Wherever the African is, there is his religion; he carries it to the fields where he is sowing seeds or harvesting a new crop; he takes it with him to the beer party or to attend a funeral ceremony; and if he is educated, he takes religion with him to the examination room at school or in

the university; if he is a politician he takes it to the house
of parliament. ...African people do not know how to exist
without religion. (Mbiti, 1990, p. 2)

The African world view also maintained a fundamental unity between the spiritual world and the material
world. Religion and nature were one. Africans always
sought a balance and rhythm in this unity (Nobles,
1980). Thompson (1981) found evidence of this overrid-
ing theme in his investigation of the art of numerous
African tribes. Herskovits (1941) confirmed this unity in
his descriptions of the integration of song and dance in
the Dahomean, Gold Coast choruses, the Shango cult
songs of Trinidad and the Brazilian Negro melodies.
Across the diaspora, wherever large groups of Africans
reside, even now, there is evidence of the theme of unity
- balance and rhythm. Unity could clearly be seen in the
African kinship system as well as in the music which was
used to create and strengthen the corporate feeling and
solidarity (Mbiti, 1990, p. 67).

Kinship Was Important

In the African kinship system, the tribe gave identity
to the individual. The individual was part of the collective
unity, a participant in collective responsibility. Whatever
happened to the individual happened to the tribe.
Solidarity and community life were esteemed. African
self-concept derived from the statement "... I am because
we are and because we are, therefore, I am" (Nobles, p.
29). To Africans, everybody is related to everybody else,
and they referred to one another with kinship terms:
"brother," "uncle," "nephew," "sister" (Mbiti, 1990, p.
102).

In her text on African roots, culture and learning
styles of Black children, Hale-Benson (1986, p. 69)
suggests that, as a result of the African kinship system
that governs child-rearing practices, Black children tend
to be more feeling-oriented and people-oriented than
their White counterparts.

Time Was Symbolic

To Africans, the concept of time was always related
to an event rather than a mathematical moment. A

27

meeting that took place at sunrise could occur at 5 a.m. or at 7 a.m. as long as it was within the general period of sunrise. The meeting took place whenever most of the people got there (Mbiti, 1990, p. 19). As a modern counterpart, Hale-Benson (1986) describes the term CPT or "Colored People's Time" as an African American expression that is used jokingly to mean approximate time rather than exact time. CPT can be from 20 minutes to 90 minutes later than the stated or advertised time. In the African American community, a meeting that starts late is said to start on CP time. According to Hale-Benson, similar jokes are made about time in West Africa and Jamaica (p. 16). This concept of time is seen in the African verb system that holds no future tense, as you will see in Chapter Four.

Words Carried Power

The spoken word was called Nommo by the Africans. There was magical power in the word. Sy (1989) defines it as "the primordial verb." Smitherman (1977) quotes Jahn's descriptions:

> All activities of men, and all the movements in nature, rest on the word, on the productive power of the word, which is water and heat and seed and Nommo, that is, life force itself... The force, responsibility, and commitment of the word, and the awareness of the word alone alters the world... (p. 78)

A newborn child took on meaning when his/her father whispered his/her new name in his/her ear. In African oral tradition, words accompanied medicine, death rites, and work. Words even preceded and sometimes accompanied battle. "The songs, histories, and traditions were the very soul of the tribe and were enshrined in the vernacular" (Tarynor, 1976, p. 107). Alex Haley's *Roots* described the griots as men who could recite oral histories - generations and generations of tribal events, in an effort to keep alive great deeds of their ancient kings. The griots earned their reputations as verbal performers. They were "speaking documents," who were sworn to secrecy much like those used in the Egyptian Mystery Systems. After the initiates completed a rigorous written course of study, they were permitted to learn the mysteries and prohibited from writing down the secretive teachings (*African American Baseline Essays*, 1987, p. LA-4).

A Common Deep Structure

> ...the variants of English spoken by Black communities in America and the Caribbean... exhibit a common deep structure, which has been retained like a mark and stamp upon the psyche of the Afro-American, which, at a certain level, unites Afro-Americans scattered throughout this hemisphere and the world. (Van Sertima, 1971, p. 13)

You have seen that the African world view held many connections with the language of the African American culture; the emphasis on religion, the integration of song and dance, emphasis upon time in the verbal system as an event rather than a mathematical moment, and the power of words to record historical deeds.

Deep structure is the underlying meaning in a message - the part that is not voiced but is understood by the receiver and the sender alike. All of these aspects of the African world view come together in the basic communication pattern used by most African Americans and in activities as simple as the Sunday worship service of the traditional Black Church.

Call-Response for Effective Communication

An important part of communication in the Black community is the manner in which it is delivered or the style. One of the major features of style is call-response, a requirement for effective communication. Sithole (1972), a specialist in African-derived music, claims that call-response was prevalent in African music as free and spontaneous expression.

Call-response reflects the African world view of oneness, interdependence and participation. Call-response seeks to bring together the speaker and the listener in a unified movement. Smitherman (1977, p. 104) defines call-response as a "...spontaneous verbal and nonverbal interaction between speaker and listener in which all the speaker's statements (calls) are punctuated by expressions (responses) from the listener." The response may occur *during* the call or *immediately after* the call is given. Response provides acknowledgment, without acknowledgment, communication does not exist. Asante (1987) calls these responses affirmations.

Here are two examples. Read this sentence aloud and say the underlined word twice: In the beginning was the Word. The first part of the sentence was the call, and the repetition was the response. Now, read the sentence again and stop at was. This is what the call would be. The responder would finish the sentence with "the word".

In call-response, both parties talk and both parties listen. There is an emotional synergism with affirmation. Speakers give one another constant feedback so they can mutually assess the effectiveness of their performance. The speaker has the *responsibility* of issuing the call, and the listener has the *obligation* to respond in some overt way - by smiling, laughing, nodding, rocking side to side, hitting the desk, or saying something like "Amen" or "uh-huh" to confirm agreement or disagreement. Responses will vary according to the individual, who will be talking both during and after the speaker speaks. The only wrong response is no response. There is *no* communication without acknowledgment.

The European world view holds another sharp contrast: one who "listens" to a speaker does so by sitting quietly, looking at the speaker and rarely displaying an outward sign or response. It is impolite to talk when someone else is talking. According to Kochman (1981), Whites (European Americans) consider continuous feedback in conversation as a constant source of interruption.

African classical music or jazz, popular music, rock, and rap all have numerous instances of call-response. Call-response was common in the slaves' songs. Dodson and Ross (1977) report that the basic structure of blues music is A-A-B, the call-response pattern. Nichols (1989) found this kind of "participation" a distinctive feature of storytelling styles of African American children as opposed to what she called "distance" that was distinctive of European American children. Taylor (1987) has found that African American children in their storytelling are likely to link a wide range of topics in a temporal sequence, emphasize showing rather than telling and presume a shared knowledge with the listeners. So, call-response has even been reflected in the writing style of children of the African American culture. Call-response is the leader's way of establishing and maintaining rapport with his/her audience.

The African world view is perpetuated in the worship service of the traditional Black church. Just as religion was the center of African life, so it also is in the life of many African Americans. Throughout the service, orality is extremely important.

Language and the Traditional Church Service

The traditional Baptist church offers an excellent example of the cultural connections described in Hilliard's quote at the beginning of this chapter. The entire church service reflects the African world view through language and communication: the emphasis on religion, the importance of kinship, the symbolic concept of time, the magical power of the word, and call-response for effective communication. African connections can be made throughout - from the music to the prayers to the sermon and even the food eaten in fellowship after service.

Before the regular worship service begins, there is Prayer Service, directed by the deacons, who lead the congregation in songs and prayers and testimonials. Prayer Service is designed to evoke the Holy Spirit. The deacons lead by "lining the hymn" (reading the hymn line by line with the people singing after each line is given). They are giving the call. Those members of the choir present and the congregation respond - they join in singing - a cappella - after each line is presented.

Father, I stretch my hand to thee, No other help I know,
If thou withdraw thyself from me, Ah, whither shall I go?
(Townsend, 1973, p. 201).

The initial song is followed by the offering of prayer by the deacons - the elders of the church who pray on behalf of the people (Mbiti, 1990, p. 69). Accompanying the prayer are always responses from the audience which compare to Sithole's description of African element "...of unrehearsed and uninhibited performances by the audience" (p. 78). Individuals may *testify* (a verbal strategy) during this service by telling how thankful they are for "...what the Lord has done for me! Church, He can make a way out of no way..." and the person may continue with a personal testimony about something the Lord has done for her. She may end by leading a song, which the congregation would join in singing. The deacons' prayers always begin the same way, by the issuing of a call. The congregation's response is shown in parentheses.

> Lord, it is once again and another time your handmaid servant comes before you to say "thank you" (the congregation says "thank you"), I thank you for my last night's lying down, that it was not in vain (an individual might say "Thank you, Lord") and the angels that watched over me all night long while I slumbered and slept. (Congregation: "Yes, Lord") And early (members of the Congregation at separate times: "early, early, Lord") early this morning, You touched me with Your finger of love. I woke up, clothed in my right mind, in a cool world and a gospel land, (Congregation: "Yes, Lord, gospel land") with the blood still running warm in my veins. I had the activity of my limbs, and You started me out on another day's journey. I just want to say "Thank you, Lord" (Congregation: "Thank you, yes, yes, yes, thank you").

The prayer continues with requests to bless the church "from the pulpit to the door," most especially "the Shepherd, to crown his head with wisdom and knowledge," "the sick, shut in, the elderly and the widowed," and finally "... when it's your time to *call* and my time to *answer*..." the deacon asks for "... a home somewhere in the kingdom". All requests are made in Jesus' name.

A conversation with Wade Nobles (personal communication, September 17, 1990) confirms Mbiti's description that the deacon's prayer comes from the African tradition of one learned scholar or elder offering prayer for the group. Smith (1974, pp. 98,183) describes "...a period of riddling "... in the African oral tradition that precedes all storytelling sessions. He calls this "testifying" a very distinct feature of the Afro American Baptist, Methodist, and Holiness churches during which members "...stand and make a personal avowal of faith and belief in God."

There is no specific time limit on the church services, especially on Communion Sunday. The crowd is sparse for Prayer Service and at the beginning of the regular worship hour, but by the time the minister brings his sermon, everyone who is supposed to be there is in attendance. (This reinforces Mbiti and Nobles' description of time associated with an event rather than mathematical moment.)

The minister "takes his text" by reading a specific passage from the scripture. He uses vivid descriptions, offers numerous examples and admonishes the congregation to do what "thus saith the Lord." As the minister preaches, his words are punctuated with *responses* from the congregation: "Amen", "Yes Lord", "Say it, Reb, (Reverend)" and other overt expressions. There is always an effort to be on one accord (the world view of unity). Those ministers who are most adept at talking and singing receive the heaviest *response*, in terms of "amens". In fact, the preacher chastises the congregation with "Can I get a witness?" or "You don't hear me, do you?" if he does not receive adequate response to an appropriate point at which he has made the *call*. According to Sithole (1972, p. 81), this same request for feedback occurs in soul music and in public speeches given by African Americans.

As the choir sings, they sway from side to side and so does most of the congregation. At many points, the entire church seems to be swaying in unison. The preacher opens the doors of the church by issuing a *call* to the congregation. (Holt, pg. 198). There is great rejoicing when an individual, who has decided to join the church, *responds to the call.*

The service is considered "good" if the spirit is high, and if the minister hits the consciousness of the people with his sermon. Throughout the sermon, there is much oral participation, improvisation, and spontaneity. People "get happy" by shouting, crying, falling out and/or exhibiting spiritual visitation. Others join in by singing, hand-clapping, foot stomping, and rocking from side to side (spontaneous expression from Sithole's description).

The service is upbeat. Church is often viewed as a place where people assemble to recharge their batteries so that they can deal with their daily problems throughout the following week. Mbiti (1990, p. 72) reports that group gatherings to solicit God's help serve to strengthen, encourage, and make suffering easier to bear.

On special Sundays, such as Homecoming and Men's and Women's Day, when large numbers of visitors are expected at the church, dinner is served. On most occasions, the menu consists of fried chicken, roast turkey and gravy, candied yams, rice, butter beans, collard greens, string beans, cornbread, and (sweet) potato pie and pound cake for dessert. Every woman brings her tastiest covered dish. There is much talking, sharing of recipes, and general conversation and laughter among those who fellowship at the (dinner) table. The members address one another as "Brother" and "Sister." Every morsel of food is savored - even down to the "pot likker" - the juices from the collard greens.

In the preparation of food, the theme of unity or interrelatedness is perpetuated. The thick sauces or gravies are used to integrate the flavors of a dish ensuring that all who taste even a morsel can savor the main dish (Dodson and Ross, pp. 29-30).

The pervasiveness of the culture can be seen in the work of several African American authors who have described similar church experiences. James Comer, (1988) Yale psychiatrist in his best seller, *Maggie's American Dream* paints a picture of the traditional church experience as he recalls the most memorable events of his childhood in Chicago. Holt's (1972) and Burling's (1973) descriptions are almost identical. Smitherman (1977) makes numerous references to the church by emphasizing that it is the center of African American culture, because it has represented a sustaining force in the face of the devastating oppression of slavery.

Good things have come out of Africa - number one among them is the distinctive culture of African Americans that starts with the emphasis upon religion and extends to the theme of unity, interdependence, and oneness with nature. This world view is reflected through the language and communication patterns deeply embedded in the culture of African American people. This culture has evolved as a result of the environment and the needs of the people. It is seen in the folklore, the expressive use of language, the songs, the dance, wise sayings, secret codes, and even the food.

Culture is not only found in exotic symbols and artifacts, but in common, everyday occurrences like our worship services. I saw this very clearly as I compared the worship services in Philadelphia and Savannah. We do have a distinctive culture; whether it is in Philadelphia or Chicago or Savannah, it gives us sustenance and promotes solidarity. According to August Wilson, a two-time Pulitzer Prize-winning playwright, "...our culture was fired in the kiln of slavery and survived." It is "...still alive, it is vital and it is as vibrant and zestful as ever." Sheppard (1990, p. 8).

Many good things *have* come out of Africa! Those good things started in the written tradition and became enshrined in the oral tradition: the words, the songs, the spirituals, and even the children's stories along with verbal interactions and performances, and folk literature. We need only to examine our values, symbols, interpretations, and our perspectives in order to see these shining attributes.

This African American male demonstrates "the walk"—
the stride is rhythmic and graceful.

Both hands on the hips mean "Stop what you are doing" or "You are in BIG trouble."

CHAPTER FOUR

DISTINCTIVE FEATURES

...the crucial element to watch is not vocabulary at all, but a grammatical base, a syntactic structure. It is the African structure underlying the top layer of Anglo-Saxon words which accounts for the peculiar combinations, patterns and transformations in the speech of peoples as far apart as the Guyanese of South America, the Gambians of West Africa, and the Gullahs of Georgia (Van Sertima, 1971, p. 17).

Introduction

In Chapter Three, you saw evidence that the oral tradition of Black Communications - the words, the songs, the spirituals, verbal interactions and performances did come out of Africa. So do many of the most easily identifiable distinctive features-the syllables, the words, the phrases, the sentences, the sounds, and the intonation patterns commonly found in African American speech. You will see that there are also connections, according to Vass, who for 40 years studied the languages of Central Africa; Van Sertima, who holds degrees in African Studies, linguistics, and anthropology; and Turner, who for 15 years studied African languages and wrote a landmark publication that revealed Africanisms in the Gullah dialect. The connections link Africa, the Caribbean, and America through language. Herskovits

(1941) described BC as part of a continuum - a chain of connections starting in Africa, spreading to the Caribbean and South America and on to Jamaica and the Sea Islands and finally arriving in America. The language seems to have followed the settlement patterns of Black people across the diaspora.

The purpose of this chapter is to discuss the characteristic sounds and the structures of the language and to provide examples found in the everyday speech of African Americans. The only features I have included are those appearing most frequently in the research of respected linguistic scholars who collected data and were published in the early 60s and 70s. These records are reinforced by what I have heard in the everyday speech of African American children and adults in the last decade. Most of these features are more commonly found among Black speakers than among White speakers. Most of these features are susceptible to modification in many other languages also.

The topic of language is a very sensitive one. Some readers may take exception to the listings I have provided. I invite those readers to listen carefully to the speech of African Americans, especially those who reside in the public housing communities in large urban areas across the United States. The dialect is reinforced in these locations because in many cases, it is the only language that is used.

I also preface this discussion of distinctive features by reminding you of the three points raised in Chapter One:

1. There is a great deal of variation among BC speakers. All African Americans do not use all of the distinctive features. Certain features may be prominent in the speech of African Americans indigenous to particular parts of the country and may not be found in the speech of others. Any given speaker may not use all the features all of the time, while another may use all of the features listed plus others. One point, however, does seem true: the vast majority of African Americans *comprehend* the features.

2. Several of the features are shared with other dialects of English, including those spoken in the Caribbean, South America, the Sea Islands, the Appalachian

Mountains, and various other regions of the United States. Remember from Chapter Three, in language/dialect - different speakers interact with one another, a leveling or sharing of features occurs. Many Black speakers may sound just like White speakers of a particular region;

3. Many of the distinctive features follow a pattern, so there are definite rules that can be used to predict certain constructions. Most of the constructions and patterns are similar across the diaspora, wherever African descendants reside.

The distinctive features are not limited to syllables, words and sounds, but they also extend to *how words are used* and how they are interpreted by others. You will see this very clearly as you read Chapter Five, the discussion of verbal strategies.

Socially Stigmatized Forms

In my discussion of distinctive features, I have chosen to use only those most frequently listed by respected researchers on language renderings across the diaspora. Some researchers describe the listings as "socially stigmatized" forms, meaning those who use them are looked down upon and considered illiterate, uneducated, and/or careless in their speech. A social stigma is often considered disgraceful or nonstandard. Indeed, Black Communications has been labeled Nonstandard English - a pejorative term. I use the term Black Communications because the dialect/language is used by African descendants across the diaspora and because this way of talking is a system that not only employs a speech code, but includes speech acts, style, nonverbal behavior, sociolinguistic rules, special speaking behaviors, and moral teachings.

In American society, the further people deviate from the "norm", the more stigmatized they are. Language/dialect that is associated with people who live in the city is usually preferred over one associated with those who live in the country; language spoken by people who have middle class status has higher prestige than that spoken by working class people; and in some circles, the language of Whites is preferred over that of Blacks. Probably to some, the most socially prestigious dialect in this country is Brahmin dialect, the language of England, their mother country. (See the video tape American Tongues.) Quite naturally, those forms associated with higher prestige do not carry a social stigma, while those constructions associated with the lower prestige groups do.

According to Stice (1987, p. 16), socially stigmatized forms of English can be traced back to William the Conqueror in 1066 A.D., when he brought with him the French language, the language of the nobility and differentiated between it and Anglo-Saxon, the language of the peasants. Peasants could never aspire to a higher social position if their speech revealed their peasant inferiority.

Being Black is a social stigma in this country, so the sounds and structures of the people who use the language are also considered by some as inferior. Some forms are more highly stigmatized than others. To the people designating the social stigma, hearing certain sounds and structures is like listening to sharp fingernails scrape across a blackboard. But what is grating or funny or odd to one person can be soothing to the ears of another. So, the definition of social stigma is relative.

Distinctive Features

The Sounds

Many African American voices are easily discernible on the telephone by those who speak the same regional dialect. For example, a Northern Black can immediately identify another Black or Northern White speaker's voice. However, Northern Blacks may have some difficulty distinguishing Southern Black speakers from Southern White speakers. Many African Americans who reside in the various regions of the country speak the same dialect as White Americans. (The reverse could also be true except for smaller numbers). For instance, many Southern Black and White speakers make no distinction between the way they pronounce pin and pen. Both are pronounced /pin/. /Pin/ for /pen/ is considered an "alternation." This term is used for the special way dialect speakers say certain sounds or certain words, as you will see later.

The chart in this section presents some sound features listed by Labov (1970), Sims (1972), Burling (1973),

Smith (1974), Wolfram and Fasold (1974), Van Sertima (1976), Smitherman (1977) and Alexander (1985), who gathered examples through recordings and interviews. According to Smitherman, Black Communications employs the same number of phonemes (basic units of sound) as Standard English (SE).

Consonants

In Black Communications, consonants as opposed to vowels show the most distinctive differences. Many of the consonants of other dialects of English also have sound variability. For example, speakers from Boston, New England and New York City show similar treatments of the letter r. You may hear fort as fought and park as pahk, and cart as cot. Similarly, when listening to Southern speakers you may hear door as do-ah, and more as mo-ah.

In Figure 1, I have listed some sound features of BC and placed an asterisk in front of those forms that appear to be the most highly stigmatized. The examples have been recorded by at least three of the previously listed authors and confirmed in the examples of BC speakers with whom I come in daily contact through interviews, personal interaction, observation in conferences, on television, or through conversation with colleagues around the country.

The Th Sound.

We begin with the pronunciation of th, which in BC may sound like th, d or f depending upon its position in a word. In Standard English (SE) th has two sounds. One is voiced, the voice is heard as in this, that, these, and those. At the beginning of these words, you hear the vibration of the vocal cords as air is forced from the lungs. The other SE pronunciation of th is voiceless as in think, thick, threw, and thanks, in all of which there is no voice sound, just a sudden rush of air being forced through the teeth.

In BC, th sounds like d when the initial th sound is voiced - (as in this = dis). When the final th sound is voiceless it sounds like f as in with = wif, bath = baf, and mouth = mouf. When th is voiceless, it sounds like the

42

th in SE: <u>th</u>ick, <u>th</u>anks, and <u>th</u>irty. See Figure 1. Van Sertima (1971, p. 21) reports that there is no <u>th</u> phoneme in the African languages.

Consonant Clusters

Consonant clusters are groups of consonants that appear next to one another in words. They are usually found at the ends of words. African dialects rarely contain final or initial consonant clusters. The consonant clusters in the following words are underlined: a<u>ct</u>, a<u>sk</u>, de<u>sk</u>, sugge<u>st</u>, te<u>st</u>, and to<u>ld</u>.

In BC, the final clusters are reduced so that the final letter is dropped. In Figure 1, I have included examples that are highly stigmatized: <u>ax</u>, <u>des</u>, <u>ghos</u>, <u>lis</u>, <u>tes</u> and <u>was</u>. When BC speakers pluralize these words, they follow the regular rules of pronunciation by adding -es and make <u>axes</u>, <u>desses</u>, <u>ghosses</u>, <u>lisses</u>, <u>tesses</u>, and <u>wasses</u>. Utter these words aloud in a high profile job interview and you will probably not secure that position.

The BC pronunciation of <u>ask</u> (<u>axe</u>) is very highly stigmatized. <u>Axe</u> appears in Gullah. The Oxford English Dictionary lists <u>axe</u> as the literary form used until about 1600. In fact, <u>ax</u> for <u>ask</u> is still used today in England as well as in Midland and Southern dialects and also in Ulster, a province of Northern Ireland.

The letter <u>r</u>.

The <u>r</u> that follows a vowel is one of the most variable features of English pronunciation. As you saw in the introduction to this section on pronunciation, regional pronunciations of <u>r</u> include <u>fort</u> as <u>fought</u>, <u>park</u> as <u>pahk</u>, <u>cart</u> as <u>cot</u>, <u>door</u> as <u>do-ah</u>, and <u>more</u> as <u>mo-ah</u>. The <u>r</u> in BC is also lost or omitted so that you might hear the highly stigmatized forms of <u>door</u> as <u>doe</u> and <u>court</u> as <u>coat</u>. Now, when the letter <u>r</u> is spoken - as when someone is spelling a word -<u>r</u> is exaggerated. Art is spelled orally as "<u>a</u>" - "<u>arah</u>" - "<u>t</u>." This appears to be a hypercorrection. A hypercorrection is defined by Smitherman as an "overly correct" form. In an effort to be correct, the speaker uses the rule, but applies it too many times. In this case, the speaker overcompensates by placing stress on the spelling of the letter <u>r</u>.

Alternation of str/skr.

The pronunciation of skr for str as in scratch for stretch is another highly stigmatized dialect feature discussed in Chapter Two. In an effort to determine its distribution, I interviewed 218 nine and ten year olds on free lunch rolls of schools in Georgia and South Carolina. Many children who use the alternation had been referred to speech classes to "correct" this dialect feature.

Sims (1972) lists this as a phonological feature in her dialect study of informants in Detroit. Contrary to the findings of Wolfram and Fasold (1974) who said it occurred in the speech of younger children and was given up automatically as they grow older, and Labov (1970), who concluded that it was common in Negro speakers in South Carolina, I found this to be a distinctive dialect feature used by African Americans. I also found a continuum that may indicate sound change in progress. If children said skretch for stretch, they probably used the skr alternation in other words that contained the feature: skreet for street, skrong for strong, skrike for strike, skranger/deskroy for stranger/destroy. There were some who said skreet but did not make the alternation on other words with that sound.

According to Smith (1974) and others, one of BC's most Africanized features is letter patterns in words. African phonology maintains a consonant-vowel-consonant pattern in words. This pattern is clear in two-syllable words that end in ing, the final g is not stressed, and becomes -in', as in lookin', runnin', walkin', and singin'.

Vowels

In BC, vowels are usually varied to show emphasis. Smitherman includes "Sang good, now y'all", meaning "sing good" (p. 18). Other vowels also are emphasized. For instance, hungry pronounced as hongry in "I'm hongry," means "I'm famished" rather than just "ready to eat." The use of voice inflections (highs and lows in pitch) can communicate beyond the letters in a word, or the words in a phrase or sentence. For instance, mmh humm (meaning yes) can indeed mean yes, unless one is skeptical, and then mmh humm uttered as a doubtful sound can mean "I'm not so sure about that." By the same token, tone can also communicate beyond the surface structure of a sentence. For instance, if a speaker asks, "You gon' eat all that food?", She means, "You really do not need to eat all that food." That question can be accompanied by a direct stare from the speaker.

Figure 1

Some Phonological (Sound) Features of Black Communications

Feature	Example	Notes
initial th can become d	*them – dem *then – den *this – dis *those – doz	th may be pronounced as d when the initial sound is voiced
final th becomes f	with – wif bath – baff both – boaf Ruth – roof south – souf mouth – mouf birthday – birfday	th may sound like f when the ending sound (th) is voiceless Burling (1973) describes this alternation as widely noted but relatively unimportant
final consonant clusters are reduced	act – ak told – toll/toe *ask – axc *desk – des *wasp – was *test – tes *list – lis *ghost – ghos	Loss of the final consonant is common when the word ends in s plus a consonant. The earliest written pronunciation of ask was axe
Pluralization of deleted clusters	*asks – axes *desks – desses *ghosts – ghosses *lists – lisses *tests – tesses *wasps – wasses	Pluralized forms of words ending in -s, follow the regular rule by adding -es: bus to busses

Deletion of r after a vowel	*door = doe fort = fought *pour = paw/poe (fear = fair) *four = foe star = stah more = moe during = doing *court = coat *their = they (in "She talkin' 'bout they momma") *We're = We (in "We ready now, let's go.")	Deletion is evident in White speakers of England, Boston, New York City. The r that follows a vowel is highly variable in SE.
Alternation of skr for str	*stretch = skratch *strong = skrong *street = skreet stranger = skranger destroy = deskroy	This form, also found in Gullah (see Dandy, 1988), is used by some speakers who were born in the South
Dropping of final g in two syllable words ending in ing	looking = lookin' living = livin' talking = talkin'	Smith (1974) lists this form as a consonant-vowel-consonant phoneme pattern (p. 107)
Vowel sound plus ng, nk - can change to show emphasis	drink = drank thing = thang think = thank ring = rang sing = sang (Examples: Do yo thang! They can sang!	Vowels can change for special emphasis (from Smitherman, p. 18)

*Indicates this form is highly stigmatized.

Dialectal Homophones

The most significant part of the pronunciation features of BC occurs in the homonyms or homophones, defined as words that have the same pronunciation but are spelled differently, such as to/two/too and there/their. Many of the distinctive and stigmatized sound features of BC sound like other words because of dialectal pronunciations. For instance, the th in then could be pronounced d, so that then and den become homophones and so do Ruth and roof, ask and ax, told and toll or toe, court and coat.

There are numerous other examples of homophonous pronunciations that are attributed to dialect features. Although the pronunciations may be the same, the context or setting in which the words are used will determine what the words are. Teachers should be aware of the sound features of BC so that they will be able to help students differentiate between two totally different words. [Miscommunications can occur between two dialect-different speakers if they are not aware of one another's dialectal homophones.] Chapter Seven will discuss further educational implications. Here is the beginning of a growing list of homophonous pronunciations.

Homophonous Pronunciations
(BC)

(Words that could be miscues)

ask – ax	weather – rather
court – coat	stream – scream
during – doing	stretch – scratch
oil – all	stroll – scroll
Ruth – roof	then – den
	told – toll

The Structure

According to Smitherman (1977), Burling (1973), and Van Sertima (1971), the greater differences between Standard English and Black Communications occur in the grammar, which is least likely to change over any period of time. Incorrect grammatical forms are highly stigmatized. Even in the African American community, those who "split verbs" for example, "He run in a race" are regarded as the most serious violators of "the King's English." Evidence that this sentiment has been around for a long time can be seen in Levine (1977), who documented Sea Island tales of African Americans in 1919 stressing the need for clear, well-enunciated speech. Indeed, many of the most highly stigmatized forms can be traced to the African languages.

Morphemes

Morphemes are the smallest units of meaning. The letter -s has meaning, but it cannot stand alone. -S and -ed are two of the most important and frequently used

47

suffixes in English. They can be added to nouns and verbs. But, they are a source of confusion for native English speakers as well as for those who speak English as a second language. Turner (1985) reports that for Black college students whom he has taught, failure to affix -s and -ed is the most frequent error. At the college level this is a concern and some schools have taken steps to assist African American students. For example, San Josè State University's Writing Center has published a handout that provides excellent coverage of -s and -ed word endings.

Pluralization

Let us begin with the letter -s. As a unit, -s can mean "more than one." If you add the suffix s to the end of a noun, it makes the word plural:

> There is one book on the table.
> There are three books on the chair.

The numbers [two, three, five, etc.] and verb forms such as are and were can also indicate plural. Standard English (SE) is highly redundant - it says the same thing more than one way in the same sentence. The second sentence above has indicated plural in three ways at once: are, three and the -s on books.

Internal change can also show that a noun is plural. (The dictionary usually shows the plural form of nouns.)

> This woman is my mother.
> These women are my aunts.

Pluralization in Black Communications is usually shown once, so that nearly all nouns have the same form whether singular or plural. See Figure 2.

> Two boy just left.
> Now, I got five cent.

Sometimes you may hear an African American use "womens." This is another example of a hypercorrection. Other hypercorrections include the following:

> Them churn (or chil-rens) driving me crazy.
> Tell the peoples it's they time.

Turner (1949) and Van Sertima (1971) report that nouns also remain unchanged in Gullah and the African languages Ibo, Kango, Ewe, Ga, Efik, and Yoruba. Van Sertima's Gullah example is "Den you cud git a yaad of clawt fuh <u>tree cent</u> uhr <u>five cent</u>" (p. 17), which translates as "Then you could get a yard of cloth for three cents or five cents."

The chart below summarizes syllabic forms of BC:

Figure 2

Stigmatized Syllabic Forms

Feature	BC Example	BC Rule	SE Counterpart
Pluralization with <u>-s</u>	Now, I got five <u>cent</u>. Two <u>boy</u> just left.	Plurality is expressed once in a sentence, usually by number.	Plurality can be expressed in the noun, the verb and the adjective. There <u>are five yards</u> of cloth. <u>These women are</u> my <u>sisters</u>.
Possession shown by <u>-s</u>	She over <u>Mary</u> house. This is <u>Larry</u> book.	Possession is shown by proximity - the owner's name precedes the object owned	One way of showing possession is to add <u>'-s</u> to the noun. She went to Mary<u>'s</u> house.
Third person singular present tense <u>-s</u>	He <u>go</u> everyday. The man <u>want</u> to run.	Verbs usually retain the same form in person and number.	SE requires <u>-s</u> on third person singular present tense: sing.: he, she or it goe<u>s</u> plur.: they go
Use of <u>-ed</u> in past tense	He <u>say</u> it to me yesterday. Then he <u>start</u> crying. She <u>lookded</u> tired. (hypercorrecction)	Verbs usually retain the same form in all tenses	Regular verbs add <u>-ed</u> to indicate past tense. Today I look. Yesterday I look<u>ed</u>.

Possession

The <u>-s</u> morpheme can also be added to a noun to show possession. This form is usually written with an apostrophe ['], either before or after the letter -s.

> That child's father is my uncle.
> The Harris' home was on fire.
> The children's supper is on the table.

The BC rendition of those sentences would show possession by proximity. The name of the owner precedes the person or object owned (Burling, 1973). You can tell by the context of the sentence who or what is owned.

> That chile father my uncle.
> The Harris home catch on fire.
> Them churn supper on the table.

The pronoun their is also used to show possession. In BC, their becomes they and possession is shown by the position of the words.

> I'm gonna tell they mother.
> I'm gonna tell they daddy, too.

The Gullah example "fo yuh git to dat girl house," translated as "before you get to that girl's house," and uses a similar possessive form (Van Sertima, 1971 p. 17).

Third-Person Singular

The morpheme -s also indicates third person singular of the present tense verb. The letters -es are added to those words ending in -s, -z, -x, -ch or -sh. In Standard English, -s on present tense verbs often indicates habitual action or action that occurs over and over. It is used only with singular third person pronouns he, she, it and with singular nouns, never with the first and second person pronouns I and you. It is never used with a verb which has a helping word: she can sing, he will sing, it might break.

Here is the verb to want conjugated in the present tense. Notice, in Standard English the morpheme -s is only used in third person singular. This differentiation is an irregularity, since no suffix is used to mark present tense with other persons.

Figure 3

Third Person Singular
SE Conjugation (BC Counterpart)

Person	Singular	Plural
1st Person speaking	I want (I want[s]	we want (we want)
2nd Person spoken to	you want (you want)	you want (you want)
3rd Person spoken about	he, she, it wants (he, she it want)	they want (they want[s])

BC verbs are marked for person within the context of the sentence by using the singular on plural subject.

I loves my baby.
He do it like that all the time.
She want to buy you a necklace. They gots to get it done.
They docsn't want anything she have.

The irregularity of differentiating third person singular can be seen as foreign language speakers attempt to regularize the verbs. The Gullah verbs show no distinction in form: What bark heah bite yonder (Van Sertima, 1971, p. 141).

Past Tense

In English, -ed indicates the past tense, action that is completed.

When I came home, he started crying. He said it to me yesterday.
She looked tired.

Start and look are "regular verbs" - they form the past tense by adding -ed: started, looked. Most irregular verbs show past tense through some internal change that involves a new sound as well as a different spelling. The dictionary lists past forms of verbs. Here are some common irregular forms:

Present Tense	Past Tense
say	said
do	did
eat	ate
tell	told
see	saw
hit	hit

BC usually makes no differentiation in verb forms in the past tense, but other words in the sentence indicate that action has been completed:

> I look for him <u>last night</u>. (Smitherman, p. 26).
> <u>When I came home</u>, he start crying.
> He say it to me <u>yesterday</u>.

The West African languages such as Ewe use a "verbal complex" - another word to show that an action is completed (Van Sertima, 1971, p. 141).

The Verb "To Be"

In English, the verb <u>to be</u> has several forms - <u>is</u>, <u>are</u>, <u>am</u>, <u>was</u>, and <u>were</u> - that vary according to the tense of the verb and the person and number of the subject. Here is an example of sentences that use the conjugation of the verb <u>to be</u> in six tenses.

Figure 4

Tense	SE Sentences using form of the verb <u>to be</u>.
Present:	The coffee <u>is</u> cold.
Past:	The coffee <u>was</u> cold.
Future:	The coffee <u>will be</u> cold.
Present Perfect:	The coffee <u>has been</u> cold.
Past perfect:	The coffee <u>had been</u> cold.
Future perfect:	The coffee <u>will have been</u> cold.

In BC, use of the verb <u>to be</u> is highly stigmatized. This verb form can either be used or be omitted to allow for two different translations. Its meaning is determined by the context.

Smitherman (1977) contends the use of <u>be</u> (also written bees or be's) in BC is one of its most distinctive features. Wolfram and Fasold (1974) term this the "invariant be" and consider it a source of misunderstanding by SE speakers. Burling (1973) describes it as a contracted form of is and are that is deleted in Black Communications. [It is interesting to note that the Russian language does not use an equivalent of the English verb to be.]

Be/Non-Be

Smitherman's (1977) discussion of the be/non-be rule describes the forms using be as showing a condition that is an everyday occurrence - repeated action. For example, He be tired means that he is always tired, or Everyday he is tired. Smitherman's description of the use of bees in the example below can allow for several translations and can encompass several tenses in one utterance, depending on the context.

Figure 5

BC Rendition	SE Translations
The coffee bees cold.	The coffee is cold.
	The coffee was cold.
	The coffee will be cold.
	Everyday the coffee is
	cold. (Smitherman, p. 19).

Baxter's (1986) version 1 of "*Shirley and the Valentine Card*" provides additional examples of the use of be to show continued action.

All the children Shirley be with in school like her, too...
...she start to liking him so much she be scared of him (p. 88).

Be, in the first sentence, indicates that Shirley is with these children on a continuing basis. She be scared means she is afraid of him whenever she is around him.

When be is omitted, the condition is temporary. Burling (1973, p. 53) compares this deletion of the be to SE contractions. While SE has two possibilities - the full and contracted form - BC adds a third form - deleted.

Figure 6

Three Forms

Full form	Contracted form	Deleted form (BC)
The coffee is cold.	The coffee's cold.	The coffee cold.
He is going.	He's going.	He going.
We are hungry.	We're hungry.	We hungry.

Smitherman's example and translations are applicable here:

> The coffee cold.
> Today the coffee is cold.
> It might not be cold tomorrow.
> It might not have been cold yesterday. It's cold today.
> (p. 19)

Be can be deleted before nouns, pronouns, adjectives, adverbs, prepositional phrases, and in auxiliary constructions (Smitherman, 1977). Baxter's Black vernacular version of *"Shirley and the Valentine Card"* provides several examples.

Figure 7

BC Example	SE Translation
She a nice girl.	She is a nice girl (noun)
She act like she his...	She acts like she's his (pronoun)
She worried...	She is worried (adjective)
She so worried...	She is so worried (adverb)
He in her class...	He is in her class (prepositional phrase)
Everything going to be alright...	Everything is going to be alright. (auxiliary)

The Center for Applied Linguistics has developed a videotape that *describes speech* in New Orleans. Its title is "Yeah you rite," an example of BC that omits the verb "to be." The SE translation is "Yes, you are right." The absence of the verb to be indicates a temporary condition: "Yes, you are correct right now. Tomorrow you may be wrong."

The use of be can also indicate future time. For the

sentences below, the SE speaker would merely insert <u>will</u> before <u>be</u>.

> The boy <u>be</u> here soon. (future be)
> They family <u>be</u> gone Friday. (future be)
> I <u>be</u> practicing every day. (future be)

Mbiti (1990, pp. 16-19), an African scholar of religion and philosophy, reports that in the East African languages he studied, no words exist to illustrate the idea of a distant future. This idea is related to the African concept of time, which becomes meaningful at the point of the event rather than at a mathematical moment.

> ...according to traditional concepts, time is a two-dimensional phenomenon, with a long past, a present, and virtually no future. ...The future is virtually absent because events which lie in it have not taken place, they have not been realized and cannot, therefore constitute time.

Van Sertima (1971, p 21) maintains the concept of time among the Bantu places the emphasis upon the *mode* of action rather than the time of action. As previously described in BC by Smitherman, action indicated is either habitual, completed, conditional, or obligatory.

Turner (1949, p. 225) confirms that Gullah uses the same form of the verb to refer to present, past and future. One form used with <u>been</u>. "What you been do?" Is similar to the English "What have you been doing", but could also mean, What did you do? - What were you doing? - What have you done? - What had you done? - What had you been doing?

Been

The use of <u>been</u> in BC is also based on the context of the sentence. Smitherman (1977, p. 21-23) offers a very thorough discussion of three uses of <u>been</u>. Generally, wherever SE uses <u>have</u>, <u>has</u>, or <u>had</u> plus <u>been</u>, BC uses only <u>been</u>. <u>Been</u> is used in BC to show past action that has recently been completed.

Smitherman offers these examples.

BC Use of Been	SE Counterpart
He been there before.	He has been there before.
They been there before.	They have been there before.
She been there and left before I even got there.	She had been there and left before I even got there. (1977, p. 22)

Based again upon the context of the sentence, <u>been</u> can also be used with other verb forms to show past action recently completed or completed at a later time.

BC Use of BEEN to show past action

I <u>been</u> had that job.
She <u>been</u> told him she needed the money.
He <u>been</u> had that scar.
We <u>been</u> lived here.
They <u>been</u> fixed the door. (Baugh, 1983, pp. 80, 81)

<u>Been</u> is used for stress to emphasize an action that has already occurred whether just recently or a long time ago. In these sentences, no other expression of time is needed (Smitherman). According to Baugh (1983) there is evidence that this stressed "BEEN" is used in Caribbean varieties of Creole English.

I BEEN ready to go. (For quite a while, now, I have been ready, and I wish you would get ready, too.) Chile, he BEEN gone. (Didn't you know that he has been gone for a long time.) They BEEN married. (They have been married for quite a while now.)

The Words

According to Smitherman (1977, p. 43) the semantics (words) used in Black Communications evolved from four sources:

1. Words of direct African origin;
2. Words that arose as a result of servitude and oppression;
3. Words that derived from music and cool talk; and
4. Words that originated in the Black church.

Smitherman (1977, p. 72) also contends that there exists an "...Afro-Americans' intuitive knowledge of

Black Semantics..."that allows Blacks from various regions of the country to understand and interpret "...any words, expressions and idioms not heard before..." This ability to understand is the common deep structure shared by those within the culture (Smith, 1974, p. 101).

Words of Direct African Origin

Turner (1949) pointed out 4,000 words he called "Africanisms" in the Gullah dialect. His final chapter also provides Gullah narratives that allow for further study and direct comparison with other languages. In addition to numerous Gullah personal names from West African words, Turner includes benne, the sesame; sack from nsake, a bag or sack; o from o la wo, an exclamation indicating surprise or anxiety; nana from na, nna, a term of respect used to address an aged woman; pat from pat meaning to keep silent.

Dalby (1972 pp. 170-186), a reader in West African languages, provides more than 80 Africanisms in American English, along with the language designation and definitions. He includes cula as in ooca-cola from Temne, okay meaning all right, used widely in West African languages Mandingo, Wolof, Dogon, Djabo, Western Fula and also in Jamaican English; say and says from Mandingo and also used in Caribbean English; tote - to carry from Western Bantu languages Kikongo, - tota which means "to carry".

Vass (1979) points out distinctive African place names in Southern states, in folktale and songs and vocabulary words appearing in dictionaries and in the writings of Americans. Vass investigated words in terms of their documented American origin and compared the words for meaning similarity as well as sound resemblance to African words. She confirmed modern linguistic unity among Africans. "In modern Africa... a Tshiluba- speaker has enough basic vocabulary in common with Kikongo, Lingala, Swahili, and Lwena to make himself understood in widely scattered cities" (p.100).

According to Vass, primary importance was given to names as well as nicknames, because they preserved the spirit of dead family members whenever those names are given to newborn children. Vass compares and contrasts African naming customs with those of Native Americans.

Naming customs of the latter groups usually describe nature: <u>bak</u> (creek), <u>hacha</u> (river), <u>oka</u> (water), <u>ushi</u> (cane), whereas African place names relate to human or social situations: <u>Tshibum bula</u> (the great destruction), <u>Molonda Mbuju</u> (followed the goat), <u>kanyinganyinga</u> (sadness) and <u>kolemashika</u> (it really got cold p. 102).

Vass describes slave importation details and lists more than 200 place names in six Southern states: Florida, Mississippi, North Carolina, Georgia, South Carolina (42% are here) and Virginia. Among them are the following place names: <u>Congo</u> from Kongo a Bantu tribe that occupies the area where the Zaire River flows into the Atlantic Ocean; <u>Echota</u> from <u>A Tshiota</u> meaning the clan or belonging to the extended family group; <u>Suwanee</u> from <u>(n) Sub-wanyi</u> meaning my house; <u>Yock-anookany</u> from <u>yaka</u>, <u>nukana</u> meaning go make a fetish; <u>Angola</u> from <u>Angola</u> the African coast from which large numbers of slaves were shipped; <u>Peedee</u> from <u>Mpidi</u>, meaning dark cloth worn during mourning; and <u>cash</u> from <u>Kasha</u>, a place in Zaire.

Here are additional words in Vass' list of possible Bantu origins:

Figure 8

Word	African Original	African Definition
banjo	<u>mbanza</u>	stringed instrument
batra, battra batten	<u>batta</u>	beat, pound something on a hard surface
catawampus (askew, awry)	<u>Katakan kula</u>	hang unevenly, one side long
diddy-wa-diddy	<u>wadia-wadia</u>	you eat and eat
gumbo (southern dish of okra, corn, butter beans, etc.)	<u>Kingumbo tshingombo</u>	okra
company	<u>omping</u>, <u>kompe</u>	peer, companion
so-so	<u>soso</u>	just nothing but
humbug	<u>humbug</u>	tease, bother, annoy

Words of Servitude and Oppression

Holt (1972) contends that Blacks practice "inversion" with the language. They reverse the meanings of particular words to manipulate and deceive Whites. This process, Holt claimed, was a defense mechanism designed to help them withstand oppression and servitude and promote group solidarity. The listener must listen closely to the tone of the voice as well as the context to understand what is meant.

> Adapting to an unbearable and unbeatable system... necessitated the production of a special form of communication interaction between master and slave. Blacks were clearly limited to two responses: submission and subversion, since overt aggression was punishable by death (p. 152).

For instance, the term "nigger" used by Whites, is considered an insult, however, some Blacks can use the term among themselves, and it connotes affection, approval, and admiration (p. 154). Historically, spirituals sung by slaves often carried opposite meanings: plans for escape, hostile feelings toward the master, or general dissatisfaction with the oppression of slavery.

Certain other words represent sociolinguistic rules for speaking. There are derogatory terms such as Miss Ann, used to refer to all White women, particularly those who have Black people working for them; Mr. Charlie, used to refer to any White man who is over a Black man in a working position; Uncle Tom, or Tom are negative terms applied to Blacks who disclose or betray other Blacks to Whites. This term comes from the docile, unaggressive main character in *Uncle Tom's Cabin*; and *The Man*, a general term implying bitterness that is used by Blacks to refer to White men, especially policemen (Johnson, 1972, pp. 144-147). There are also terms that should be avoided: "my girl" used by Whites to refer to a Black female who is working as a domestic and "boy" used by Whites to refer to Black men. Both terms can be extremely offensive to Blacks and can provoke anger and even violence (Johnson, 1972, p. 144).

Another example of inversion is the use of the word "bad" to mean good or excellent and "bad-bad" and "super bad" to mean extraordinarily good. A popular Kentucky Fried Chicken commercial, aired during the Fall of 1990 pictured Blacks describing chicken as "bad" and the reactions of a White male, who was confused over the inversion process and thought Blacks were saying the chicken was not good. Gullah, as well as numerous African languages, used reduplicated forms in names to intensify the meanings of words such as *yoyoyo*, a name, and *trutru*, meaning *very true* (Turner, 1949, pp. 235-239).

Words from Music

The impact of African culture can clearly be seen in the music of African Americans. Indeed, African Americans have contributed to Black semantics not only through lyrics of songs, but also through the talk of musicians themselves (Smitherman, 1977, p. 53). The following terms appear on lists by Smitherman (p. 53), Dalby (pp. 177-186), Cooke (p.160) and have been derived from Black music.

cool   -   from Mandingo suma meaning slow, calm, controlled

dig   -   from Wolof deg, dega, to understand, to appreciate as in "I can dig it"

funky   -   soulful and down-to-earth sounds

hip   -   aware of what is happening and of what is appropriate

jam   -   from Wolof jaam meaning slave; to play improvised music at informal gatherings

skin   -   as in "give me some skin" meaning shake my hand, from Temne or Mandingo "put your skin in my hand"

Although some of the words listed above have outgrown their popularity, Black music, sacred as well as secular, as played by the Beatles, the Rolling Stones, and rock groups from other countries, has carried Black semantics to those foreign countries.

Street Talk

Street talk is described by Abrahams (1976) as highly stylized and unrestricted playful speech usually accompanied by a public performance. It can be used by teens as well as adults. According to Baugh (1983) "Black street speech" is situational: it is used largely by African Americans who know one another and come from the same background to establish a reputation (see Chapter Five). Foster (1986) contends that this "jive lexicon" used by teenagers causes numerous problems of communication between teachers and students. Street talk also incorporates inversion using double and sometimes triple meanings for everyday words. As you will see in Chapter Five, many of the terms used by teens change as soon as the general public understands them; however, the speech acts and events they name remain the same. Here are some of the terms included in Foster's list:

Word	Definition
bugged	annoying, crazy
chill	to take it easy
fresh	outstanding, bad
heavy	thought-provoking
homeboy or homey	best friend
lid	hat
split	to leave
tight	best of friends
waste	to beat someone up, to kill

(Foster, 1986, pp. 163-166)

Abrahams (1972 pp. 31-32) describes a kind of personal talk used by African Americans when they feel they can trust one another. Grammar, vocabulary, intonation patterns, and conversational dynamics may change depending on the situations and the topics being discussed. This talk may involve the jive lexicon listed above as well as profanity and can include such topics as "ain't White folks crazy" and "Black folks have a long way to go."

Words from the Black Church

As you saw in Chapter Three, the traditional Black church is one of the most influential institutions in the Black community. Smitherman (1977) contends that the concept of <u>soul</u> originated in the church.

> The common "church" and "street" ingredients of soul are long suffering but with a heroic posture of endurance and sheer human will to survive, knowing that "He (God) may not come when you want Him, but he's right on time, "...refusal to wallow in self-pity,...daring to show some sign" that "you got good religion" (p. 56).

Having soul extends from religion through the ability to empathize with the Black experience. It includes "digging on" the music of the number-one soul sister, Aretha Franklin, as she describes "her man"; it involves savoring the flavor of barbecue ribs, potato salad, and greens and enjoying the camaraderie of family gatherings as they reminisce about the good old days; it includes finding the will to maintain sanity and perseverance through hard times; it involves applauding the sounds and movements of MC Hammer, a popular rap star, as he blends rap and religion in his 1990 hit, "You Got to Pray Just to Make it Today." The concept of soul expands to all age groups and economic levels in the Black community.

The following words come from Smitherman's list of church-inspired terms:

Chile (child) - Affectionate term, usually used by women, to refer directly to anyone with whom he/she is talking;

Sister, Brother - forms of address for Black females and males: emphasize solidarity and unity, [still used in Africa today] (Mbiti, p. 102).

gittin' the spirit - to show deep emotion and express feeling of one's soul by body movements and gestures;

well, all right - an enthusiastic reaffirming response;

testifyin' - a ritualized form in which the speaker gives verbal witness to the efficacy, truth and power of some experience in which all Blacks have shared. Anyone can attest to the goodness of God on any occasion (p. 57).

The Sayings

An African proverb states, "To go back to tradition is the first step forward" (Warfield-Coppack, 1990). According to Mbiti (1990), African proverbs express the oldest forms of religious ideas and philosophical wisdom. These short statements are easy to remember and pass on to other people.

African American Baseline Essays (Harris, 1987, p. LA6) gives four uses for proverbs: (1) to guide human behavior, (2) to describe human nature, (3) to explain natural occurrences, and (4) to teach basic societal beliefs. Smitherman reports that proverbs serve as child-rearing devices (1977, p. 95).

The second edition of Mbiti's (1990) text on African religions and philosophy provides the following proverbs.

African Proverbs listed by Mbiti

No one shows a child the Supreme Being - Ashanti proverb meaning everybody knows of God's existence almost by instinct; even children know Him (p. 29). If God dishes your rice in a basket, do not wish to eat soup - Mende proverb meaning a person should not desire to change the state or condition in which God places him (p.41.) God exercises vengeance in silence - Banyarwandi or Barundi proverb meaning God does have punitive acts that man cannot see (p. 205).

The following proverbs are included in Smith's and Smitherman's list of Black proverbs and sayings:

It's a poor duck that won't praise his own pond - You need to have confidence in yourself.

If you lay down with dogs, you come up with fleas - If you associate with someone who has a bad reputation, you could possibly end up with that reputation too.

The price of the hat ain't the measure of the brain - Expensive clothes do not indicate intelligence (Smith, 1974, pp. 101, 102).

What goes around comes around - You reap what you sow.

A hard head makes a soft behind - Being stubborn, refusing to listen can make you pay a stiff price.

Pretty is as pretty does - You are known by your actions.

Actions speak louder than words - What you do has more relevance than what you say (Smitherman, 1977, pp. 245-246).

A chip off the old block don't fly far - children are likely to have the same characteristics as their parents.

African American Lesson Plans (Leonard, 1988) includes the following American proverbs with their African counterparts:

Into each life some rain must fall. (U.S.)
The rain falls on every roof. (African)

United we stand, divided we fall. (U.S.)
Sticks in a bundle are unbreakable. (African)

Truth wins out (U.S.)
Truth and morning become light with time. (African)
(p. 70)

Afrika (1990) lists the following Gullah proverbs (pp. 29-30).

Det wan ditch you arn fuh jump.
(Death is one ditch you have to jump.)

Er good run bettuh dan uh bad stan.
(A good run is better than a bad stand.)

Eby back is fitted to de bu'den.
(Every person is able to carry his own burden.)

Man p'int, but God disap'pint.
(Man appoints, but God is the supreme appointer.)

Nonverbal Communication

Nonverbal communication is an *essential* distinctive feature of Black Communications. Nonverbal communication is a form of body language. It is also used by BC speakers as a direct representation of a feeling. According to Cooke (1980), nonverbal communication includes giving skin, standing stances, and styles of walking. "Giving skin" and "getting skin" involves having two individuals slap one another's palms with one or both hands. This signal, usually given by males, can be symbolic of a greeting instead of a handshake; it can also be used to say hello or good-bye, to show approval or agreement, proposal or suggestion, or as a form of congratulatory response (after a touchdown at a football game or an impressive statement made by one of the individuals or even by a teacher). This interaction confirms and reestablishes group solidarity.

The standing stance, illustrated in Cooke's article, often accompanies verbal strategies such as rapping and woofing discussed in Chapter Five. These stances can also involve what Kunjufu (1986, p. 10) labels the look of defiance, "the showdown," during which the African American male stands with his arms folded sometimes diagonally across his chest and intensely stares at the teacher or another authority figure. This stance translates as "I'm bad and I know I'm bad."

Another stance can involve a lowered shoulder along with a forward lean for a male who is talking romantically (rapping) to a female, who may respond with a persistent stare and a smile, indicating her interest, or with a look away from the male rolling her eyes upward as a sign of boredom or disgust.

The most frequently appearing style of walking is very noticeable and can be considered intimidating by an unknowing observer. According to Cooke (1980), this walk is designed to attract the attention and favor of females and is usually individually executed.

> The basic soul walk consists of placing one foot directly in front of the other, the heel hits first and the leg drops loosely which results in a bent leg effect. The shoulders sway very slightly and naturally, with a slight dropping of the shoulder which moves forward. ...The overall motion is a gentle swing; the stride is rhythmic and graceful (p. 153).

This walk is seen in school hallways and on playgrounds and is used generally by males who are a part of the street culture and use street talk described in THE WORDS section of this chapter.

Discourse Routines

Another essential feature of Black Communication involves a situation that is used in social settings. A speech event is a situation that requires particular ways of speaking. The speakers are communicating in culturally specific ways. Discourse routines involve rules to which people adhere unconsciously. These routines are accompanied by performances that have been learned by speakers.

For instance, there are specific rules involved in telephone conversation. The caller waits for the receiver to say something (hello) before she asks for the person she is calling. The receiver has an *obligation* to find the person being called and to take a message if the person to receive the call is not in. In the African American community, usually whenever two middle-class African Americans meet they engage in what I call "It's a small world routine."

It's A Small World

Two African American adult males are meeting for the first time.

First speaker: Hey, man, how are you doing? What's happening...

Jim Dandy (says his name as he extends his right hand)

Second speaker: Alton Williams (Shakes hand)

First speaker: Where are you from originally?

Second speaker: Wilmington, Delaware.

First speaker: Wilmington, Delaware. That's not too far from Lincoln University.

Second speaker: Right, about 25 miles away.

First speaker: I know a guy who went to Lincoln back in the early seventies.

Second speaker: Oh, yeah, my brother went to Lincoln. What was his name?

First speaker: Harold Williams, tall guy, he played basketball for the University.

Second speaker: So did my brother. Did Williams have a gray patch in the front of his head.

First speaker: Yeah, man. He was always talking about playing pro ball.

Second speaker: Yeah, he used to come to my house with my brother.

First speaker: What's he doing now?

Second speaker: Teaching and coaching high school ball.

First speaker: Next time you see him, tell him I asked about him.

Second speaker: O.K., man. It's really a small world.

First speaker: That's right.

Second speaker: My brother will be home tonight.. Why don't you come on over?

First speaker: O.K. man, I'll be there. What time?

Second speaker: About 8:30.

First speaker: Should I bring anything?

Second speaker: No man, just yourself.

The speakers depart.

Nobles (1989) describes signs and signals used by African American females. "The evil eye" (a steady glare) focuses directly on the person who is not performing as he or she should be. It sends a silent message to "straighten up." One hand on the hips means "I'm disgusted with your behavior," and both hands mean "Stop what you are doing immediately, or you will suffer the consequences, or "you are in BIG trouble."

According to Miller (1990), 93 percent of the messages teachers send to students are nonverbal. The African American culture relies heavily on nonverbal communications, which accompany and confirm verbal communications. Teachers need to be aware of nonverbal messages sent by students to teachers. They must also be aware of the messages they send to students; especially when the verbal and nonverbal messages conflict because when inconsistent messages are sent, problems occur and students learn to mistrust the teacher. In the African American community, respect is not automatically given a person who has a prestigious title to his/her name. Respect is earned through observing the actions of an individual over a period of time. An integral part of that observation is the degree of congruence exhibited between what is said and what is not said.

Summary

The distinctive features listed in this chapter represent sounds, structures, words, sayings, nonverbal communication, and discourse routines most frequently mentioned in the literature and routinely heard during interviews and observations with African Americans. You will be hard pressed to locate any one African American who uses every single feature. I caution you not to try to fit anyone into a perfect mold or to create a perfect example. Remember, as I pointed out in Chapter One, everyone has an idiolect - his or her own personal dialect. And, that leveling or dialect sharing increases as the numbers of African Americans and Spanish Americans increase. What I do hope you have learned from this chapter is that the sounds, and the structures are consistent and logical and the language is alive and well among African Americans throughout the United States and Blacks across the diaspora. YOU AS A TEACHER MUST SEEK TO UNDERSTAND THEM AND USE THEM AS A BASIS FOR TEACHING STANDARD ENGLISH TO YOUR BC SPEAKERS.

Chapter Five will offer specific suggestions on how to approach those who use language in specific ways.

Features of BC - A Summary

SE Feature	BC Feature
Th - voiced initially in this, that, these, those - voiceless initially and finally in think, threw, birthday, cloth, math, mouth, with	th - d in words with th voiced: dis, dat, dese, dose th - f only in words and syllables ending in th: birfday, clof, maf, mouf, wif
Consonant Clusters appear at end of words and are difficult to articulate: act, ask, correct, desk, list, suggest, test, told, wasp	**Final Clusters are reduced** usually by dropping final letter: ac, axe, correc, des, lis, sugges, tes, tol, was
R is always sounded but its sound is distorted when it follows vowels as in start, we're, their, door, four	**R is omitted** at the end of one syllable words: court - coat; door - doe; four - foe; their - they; we're - we; sometimes r is pronounced "ah-rah", a hypercorrection
Str is a triple blend that occurs at the beginning or in the middle of words. All three letters are sounded	Str - Skr in stretch - skretch, strong - skrong, street - skreet
Vowels vary in sound, depending on the other vowels they follow	**Vowel sound (i)** can change to show emphasis thing - thang in "it's yo thang" sing - sang in "sang good, now"
SYLLABLES: ing even in Shakespeare's rhyme cushings was pronounced cushions and napking - napkin. This also occurs in the Southern regional dialect.	ing - in' in two-syllable words, hopin', talkin', waitin' in an effort to maintain the pattern CVCVC (consonant-vowel-consonant-vowel-consonant)
PLURALIZATION -S can be added to the end of a noun to make it mean more than one as in girl - girls; internal changes can also show plural woman - women	Plurality is expressed in a sentence - usually in the cardinal number I got five cent. Hypercorrections: chil-rens, womens

POSSESSION
-S is added to the end of a noun to show ownership

Ownership is shown by Proximity to the owner and the item owned
This Larry book.

VERBS
Third Person Singular
present tense 3rd person singluar requires an -s
He wants it

Past tense regular verbs -ed
He looked.

Verbs usually remain the same in person and in number; -s is often omitted on 3rd person singular: He want to go

Tense is reflected in a word other than the verb
He look for me yesterday.
Hypercorrection: lookded

WORDS:
Words can have a denotative - definition meaning as well as connotative meaning

Words are borrowed from particular cultures

Inversion: Meaning of particular words are reversed; bad means good, nigger can connote friendship only among Blacks, superbad means very good
African Words: coca cola, dig, yam, humbug
Words to be avoided: boy for man; girl for woman; you people for Blacks
Street talk: uses profanity, verbal strategies
Words related to music: dig, hip, cool, skin
Words related to church: sister, brother

WORD ORDER
The verb to be has forms: am, is, are, was, were, will be, been that vary according to tense and number

Omit be to show temporary condition - She tired.
Use be to show repeated action - She (always) be tired.
Use been for emphasis. I been ready.

NONVERBAL COMMUNICATION:
93% of messages sent by educators are nonverbal

Silence in response to a ridiculous question
Oculesics - eye rolling
Kinesics - side by side stance
The walk - used to impress
Signs - hands on hip, head movement, the evil eye

The sight of boisterous African American male students in a hallway makes some educators uncomfortable— sometimes fearful.

In the "showdown," the student stands with his arms folded and stares at the teacher.

CHAPTER FIVE

VERBAL STRATEGIES: RAPPIN,' WOOFIN,' AND PLAYIN' THE DOZENS

Focus on African American Males

> Among the most dramatic of all developmental events to which all youth must adjust is the host of interrelated psychological and morphological changes occurring during the early adolescent period from about 11 to 15 years of age. The term puberty derives from the Latin word *pubertas* (meaning age of manhood)... (Erikson, quoted by Mussen, Conger and Kagan, pp. 544, 557).

This chapter will examine several features of Black Communication style and speech acts as they are used by African American males during this stage of adolescence. I have chosen to focus on males for several reasons:

1. Historically, Black males have been noted for talking a particular kind of stylized talk;
2. Learning how to use this talk is an essential part of passage from boyhood to manhood;
3. Those who are successful at using this talk are often punished by schools by being referred to remedial classes, Special Education or classes for learning disabled or learning disordered; and

4. Teachers generally are unfamiliar with the rules, purpose, and intent of this stylized talk.

My intent is to sensitize teachers to the ways many Black males use words. It is my hope that teachers will subsequently be motivated to look for ways they can view these features as an asset rather than a hindrance to learning. What are essentially cultural strengths can be transferred into positive classroom experiences.

Many classroom discipline problems can be attributed to conflicts between the culture of the teacher and that of the student (Smith, 1974; Foster, 1986; Taylor, 1988; Nelson-Barber and Meier, 1990). Often students who exhibit the verbal strategies described in this chapter, are "referred" by teachers to remedial classes, special education classes or classes for behavior disorders or learning disabled. Taylor (1988) has studied this phenomenon of referring students out of regular classrooms and into "special needs" classrooms. He lists the following as most common reasons teachers refer students:

1. challenging the teacher's authority;
2. not listening quietly when the teacher is presenting the lesson;
3. interrupting another student;
4. responding in a loud voice;
5. socializing in class; and
6. using physical means to settle a conflict.

Johnson (1990) has described African American males as an endangered species! Well-documented and publicized statistics have strategically placed them at the bottom of the social totem pole - below Black females, White females, and White males - on scales including: test achievement and school behavior, but at the top of the scale in reference to remedial classes, dropouts, unemployment, crime, imprisonment, and death by violent and natural causes. Even though at birth, Black males are developmentally and mentally more alert than their counterparts, as they go through life, they fall further and further behind (Larned, 1990). There are more African American males in prison than there are enrolled in college!

Akbar (1990) acknowledges these grim findings, but contends we must not dwell on them, lest we despair.

They must be viewed within the context of the Black man's historical struggle since slavery. He cautions against the "blame the victim" mentality.

> The tendency is to begin to look at the victim as the cause of their circumstances and not the broader causes that created the circumstance. ...It begins to suggest that poverty is the cause... that a broken home is the cause... that single parent households are the cause. It begins to suggest that something is biologically or psychologically or sociologically deficient in these young people that makes them become the drug addicts, the criminals, the homicidal victims and perpetrators and begin to believe that somehow the causation is caught in the nucleus of the situation. Until we understand there has been a continuous degradation and decline of African American manhood since the first slaveship arrived in America, will we understand what's going on.--------

In an effort to endure the oppressive societal conditions, the Black male has taken the rituals initiated as manhood rites in Africa and adapted them as mechanisms for survival in a hostile land. The hidden in-group language and the verbal performance of griots (described in Chapter Three) evolved into verbal strategies.

Today, in the African American community, high value is placed upon the ability to verbalize. As a matter of fact, every time a speaker opens his mouth he is further establishing his rap or "rep" -reputation. According to Abrahams and Gay (1975) language is a means of survival that helps the user acquire status, leadership and success. It symbolizes toughness, bravery and masculinity. Orality can make the difference between

> ...having or not having food to eat, a place to live, clothes to wear, being accepted or rejected by one's peers, and being personally and emotionally secure or risking a complete loss of ego. Therefore, for a member of street culture, language is not only a communicative device but also a mechanism of control and power. It is the medium through which students learn to deal with the demands of middle class teachers without losing all semblance of self-respect (p. 159).

Abrahams and Gay's description reflects the magic

power of the word - <u>Nommo</u>. Verbal strategies are part and parcel of the skills African American males must learn in order to pass from boyhood to manhood. They are an integral part of the subculture shared by males within the Black community (Smith, 1974; Kunjufu, 1986).

Verbal Strategies

The African American male's survival in the peer group is dependent upon his adeptness at using a variety of verbal strategies. Verbal strategies are defined as the highly stylized use of words and gestures to impress, persuade, or control the audience. Names for the strategies vary according to the location and the period of time. For instance, informants who live in San Diego, report that basin' is the same as playing the Dozens; in Savannah, it is called checkin', in Washington, D.C., jonin'. See the list below for names that describe various strategies.

Figure 1

Names for Verbal Strategies

basin'	fat mouthin'	luggin'
buggin'	gum beatin'	markin'
bulldozin'	harpin'	mockin'
bustin'	hoorahin'	playin' the Dozens
cappin'	humbuggin'	rappin'
checkin'	jeffin'	shuckin' & jivin'
coppin' a plea	jibbin'	signifyin'
crackin'	jonin'	soundin'
dissin'	lollygaggin'	sweet mouthin'
dozin'	loud mouthin'	talkin' smack
droppin' lugs	loud-talkin'	testifyin'
		woofin'

Many appear in Smith's (1974) glossary of names and terms describing most of these strategies in detail.

Now these words are almost in a constant state of

flux. New words are always being developed in an effort to maintain a secret code that only the African American community's peer group understands (Abrahams and Gay). Although the names for the verbal strategies vary, the functions remain the same. The plethora of names attests to the position of importance these strategies occupy in the Black community. The appropriate use of verbal strategies is an integral part of the communicative competence of African American males. This competence involves gaining the skills that will prepare him for manhood: purpose, control, self-discipline, and independence. Verbal techniques or strategies involve the words, how the voice is used in saying the words, how the utterances are used in social settings and how others interpret their use.

This discussion will cover only three verbal strategies: rappin', woofin', and playin' the dozens. Abrahams (1963, 1972), Smith (1974), Mitchell-Kernan (1972) and Foster (1986) offer in-depth treatment and analyses of numerous other strategies.

You read about call-response in Chapter Three. It involves affirmation for effective communication between speaker and listener. In this interaction, the speaker issues a call and the listener(s) give a spontaneous response - either verbal or nonverbal. In the traditional Black church, the minister's reputation is based upon his ability to issue the call and elicit responses from the congregation. The same holds true for the African American male and his peer group: group status is based upon the youth's adeptness at soliciting responses from the audience. The only wrong response is no response.

Rappin'

Although it is enjoying a popular resurgence, rapping as a verbal strategy is an old tradition. Originally, rappin' was employed in male-female relationships as an introductory device. A male who was interested in pursuing a relationship with a female would rap to her to test her receptiveness (Abrahams and Gay, 1975, p. 160). Rappin' is "...a colorful or distinctive style of talking into which the speaker injects his personality so as to make a favorable impression" (p. 84). Kochman (1981, pp. 76-88) describes three common uses of rap:

1. To provide information to someone (runnin' somethin' down);
2. To convince or persuade someone to do something (whuppin' the game);
3. To introduce oneself (rappin' to a woman to ask for affection);

Today, we must add a fourth:

4. To entertain through music and bring a message that is played to a definite beat with the lyrics chanted rather than sung.

Any rap is highly stylized, exaggerated and flamboyant (Smitherman, 1977). Rap is accompanied by a *performance*. The rapper may use gestures, move his head from side to side, or lean one way or another. (See the Chapter on nonverbal communication). The performance/rap is good if it brings a response: a smile, a handshake (giving skin), applause, consent, wild laughter, or some other overt reaction. (This goes back to the African oral tradition that requires participatory listening discussed in Chapter Three.)

The purpose of the rap is to put the speaker in the position of control and to impress the listener. Efforts to control on the part of Black students are generally viewed as negative by the White culture, contends Kochman (1981, p. 72). Boasting and bragging label an individual as a show-off. Muhammad Ali endured a negative image in his efforts to prove that he was "The Greatest." Ali described himself with the phrase "Float like a butterfly-sting like a bee." The media downplays athletes such as Reggie Jackson who are labeled cocky.

The rapper is successful if he can absorb the audience in his conversation. As the person performs his rap, he may change the pitch and/or volume and/or rhythm of his voice, place stress on an unusual syllable, or use a range of vocal effects, such as rasp, growl, falsetto, and whine. The rapper uses active verb forms in his efforts to "throw a rap" or "run it down." His rap is filled with slang, colorful exaggerations, and incredible comparisons. This description given by Abrahams in

1972 still holds true for today's contemporary "rap" as well as for rap music. One's rap is his verbal reputation.

I remember as a teenager in the fifties, listening to a radio program out of Philadelphia that was hosted by a disk jockey named "Jocko." He would always sign on by saying:

Bee Be Bop
This is the Jock.
I'm back on the scene
With the record machine
Saying "ooh poo pee do,
How do you do"
When you up, you up
When you down, you down
When you mess with the Jock
You upside down.

Smitherman (1977) has chosen an excerpt from Richard Wright's *Black Boy* to illustrate a typical "street-corner rap." She describes how each line is delivered in parentheses.

"You eat yet?" (Uneasily trying to make conversation.)
"Yeah, man. I done really fed my face." (Casually.)
"I had cabbage and potatoes." (Confidently.)
"I had buttermilk and black-eyed peas." (Meekly informational.)
"Hell, I ain't gonna stand near you, nigger." (Pronouncement.)
How come?" (Feigned innocence.)
"Cause you gonna smell up this air in a minute!" (A shouted accusation.)
Laughter runs through the crowd. "Nigger, your mind's in a ditch." (Amusingly moralistic.)
"Ditch, nothing! Nigger, you going to break wind any minute now!" (Triumphant pronouncement creating suspense.)
"Yeah, when them black-eyed peas tell that buttermilk to move over, that buttermilk ain't gonna wanna move and there's gonna be war in your guts and your stomach's gonna swell up and bust!" (Climax.)
The crowd laughs loud and long (p. 80).

This same kind of rap and accompanying reaction can be heard in school hallways. Foster (1986) explains that some middle-class Blacks and Whites are very fearful of moving, gesturing, loud-talking rappers. Their fear of the unknown can cause negative reactions.

> When these (loud-talking and boisterous) are put together in a school hall situation of a few Black adolescents walking together, gesturing, maybe pushing and shoving one another and talking boisterously, the educators, unused to this type of physical - verbal behavior usually become very uncomfortable and, in the extreme, very fearful. Very often this leads to teacher-student confrontation and suspension (pg. 211-212).

Teachers can usually get the rappers to settle down with an appropriate professional request as in the following:

> "One morning, I was working in my office, and one of our students came in and started moving up and down and said he had to go to the lavatory. I listened, kept working, sort of ignored him, but watched him out of the corner of one eye. Finally, after a few minutes, I turned to him and said, 'No, you can't go. Your rap is weak.'
>
> He laughed and said, 'Ok, see you later.' And he tipped on back to class.
>
> From his response, it was obvious that he did not have to go to the lavatory. Whether he just wanted to get out of class, test his rap on me, or practice his rap is speculation." (Foster, 1986, pg. 210)

The teacher's reaction was appropriate for that individual. He basically communicated with the student without embarrassing him. Blowing up the issue by openly chastising the student unnecessarily detracts from instructional time. It only serves to alienate students, causing subsequent retaliation and no-win situations. Remember, peer groups are very important in the evaluation of the rap, for they must openly assess the performance.

A love rap allows any African American male to approach any female he does not know. It is a means of introducing oneself and winning the heart, affections, and mind of the female. Isaac Hayes and Barry White use this kind of rap in their vocal music. "Can't get enough of you, babe... It's like the more you give, the more I want and baby that's no lie."

Smitherman has used an example written nearly 100 years ago to illustrate the love rap. Even today, it has only to be uttered aloud by a convincing Black Male to bring a smile from a female who consents to the rap or with a quick turn of the head in the other direction indicates that she is not interested. Notice that "kin'" stands for *kind*.

> "My dear kin' miss, has you any objections to me drawing my cher to yer side and revolvin' de wheel of my conversation around de axle of your understandin'?" (*Southern Workman* Hampton Institute Folklore Collection, 1895, p. 79).

I am totally amazed at the rap music, a kind of folk music, prevalent on radio, television and in some school hallways and schoolyards today. Young people can recite detailed rhymes that carry a message with no apparent preparation and deliver them at speeds up to 200 to 250 words per minute, not missing a beat. The process has been assimilated into the advertising and entertainment industry so that even the Pillsbury Doughboy has a rap - along with Bob Hope and McDonald's. An organization entitled "Stop the Violence" (1989) has succeeded in combating the negative influence of some rap groups who use obscenities to get their points across. The members in the group Stop the Violence have dedicated their profits to using rap in positive ways to inspire young people.

The National Broadcasting Company (NBC) has recently aired a new television situation comedy that has a fun-loving, but innocent rapper as the star: "The Fresh Prince of Bel Air." The show has a significant range of idiolects exhibited by the characters: Educated English used by the mother, valley girl dialect used by the older sister, British English used by the butler and street talk used by the main character. It will be interesting to follow the progress of a show that portrays obvious cultural/language/dialect differences within the African American community. M.C. Hammer, referred to by some as the "master rapper," has won numerous music awards for his positive and highly stylized rap and performance.

Pat Pike, an educator, has also used this cultural strength to create a supplemental reading program designed to help students who have severe problems with decoding skills. *Wordbuster Reading Rap* (1987) covers long and short vowels, the consonants c and g, syllables, vowels, digraphs and silent e through a catchy rap and accompanying written and motivational activities. Pike provides step-by-step directions and music for creating additional raps and coordinating poetry writing and articulation drills through cooperative learning. She has capitalized on a strength of many students who are not succeeding in school. Used in this very positive way, rap coordinates a holistic view of language that is thought about, spoken, written, read, and shared. Rap, then continues to be a verbal strategy that is practiced, perfected and used to convince students that they too can succeed in the language arts.

Woofin'

Selling woof (wolf) tickets refers to any kind of strong language which is purely idle boasting, a form of bragging that is nearly always taken for the real thing by an outsider from another culture. Woofin' can be a form of rap. This strategy is designed to sustain anger and hostility at the verbal level, thus avoiding violence. "Through woofin', a player can maintain an image of being fearless and tough with the hope that once that image is achieved, he won't have to prove it" (Hale-Benson, 1982, p. 171).

There are usually two people involved in woofin', although there can also be an audience. Foster calls it "... telling an improbable yarn," bluffing.

To accept a challenge to fight is to accept a "woof ticket." The intent of woofin' is intimidation. In the school setting, woofin' can take these forms:

1. Standing in the hall and blocking the teacher;
2. Standing in front of a teacher or walking down the hall with a belt opened;
3. Yelling and moving one's body in a menacing way while arguing about a grade;

4. Just standing and staring at the teacher;
   Kunjufu (1986) calls this the Showdown; Cooke
   (1980) calls this the "silent rap";
5. Almost any nonverbal, verbal, or physical form of
   intimidation (Foster, 1986, p. 192).

Students can woof at one another or at the teacher. You have to be on the offensive to woof. Woofin' can also be called "doggin'," "bogarding," "loud mouthing," "loud talking," "johnin' " "sounding," or "running a strong rap." Informants from Louisville, Kentucky, and Phoenix, Arizona report that "selling woof cookies" is the same as woofin'.

Abrahams and Gay (1975), Kunjufu (1986), and Foster (1986) describe the same "woofin'" scenario.

Students themselves testify to the effectiveness of their use of language as a means of exerting power and control over the teacher and the classroom situation. Black kids claim that the middle-class teacher is "stupid," "lacks common sense," "is dumb," "naive," and that she will "believe anything." Her vulnerability and ignorance about Black life and how Black students function makes her an easy prey for students. She is so easy to "run a game on" that the exercise is hardly worth the effort (Abrahams and Gay, pg. 164).

The general rule for woofin' is that you do not woof on someone you cannot beat/frighten/intimidate. In order for woofin' to work, the person who is "woofed on" must be on the defensive and the one "selling woof tickets" must be on the offensive. The woofer has the attitude "I'm bad, and I know I'm bad." "Bad" means excellent.

Dennis Rodman, who plays basketball for the Detroit Pistons is adept at selling woof tickets. During the game, he taunts players on the other team telling them that they can't play and that they will lose the game. Muhammad Ali sold woof tickets for years when he declared as a relatively young boxer, "I'm the greatest!" He composed poetry and recited it at news conferences. Both men consistently delivered on their promises.

Now, for the middle-class female teacher, who is probably having her first direct contact with African

American males, woofin' can be terrifying. Society has painted a deviant picture of Black males through its television and newspaper portrayal of Blacks selling drugs, committing Black on Black crime, getting arrested, and filling prison cells. George Bush's 1989 presidential campaign legitimized the media's emphasis of the negative image by showing pictures of Willie Horton, the Black criminal Michael Dukakis was supposed to have released from jail. A vote for Dukakis was perceived as a vote for Willie Horton. Those who voted for Bush were expected to infer that Michael Dukakis would allow such criminals to freely walk the streets.

In the educational setting, it is Black males who are most frequently placed in the corner in classrooms, sent to the principal's office, suspended, and expelled. The negative statistics mentioned at the beginning of this chapter help to create low expectations when college textbooks and professors describe "the numerous problems" of Black people. Indeed, Dent (1989) contends that "... the negative stereotypes of Black men are locked into the psyche of the educational system," causing numerous Black children to fail. Dent quotes Kunjufu "Many of us don't realize that what happens to boys in school between the ages of 9 and 13 will determine whether they go to college or jail and how much income they will earn."

The inexperienced teacher also is at a disadvantage because the student is the expert at woofin'. In the Showdown during which the student just stands with his arms folded and stares at the teacher, the student has the advantage.

> First, he chooses the battlefield, the strategy, and the weapons, all of which involve the use of words. Second, his skills and adeptness at "keeping cool" are so well developed that they are hard to shake or to surpass (pg. 164).

Here is an example of a typical woofin' episode.

The teacher tells the student to do something and he does it, but in such a way that unnerves the teacher. He gets his way throughout the situation. Abrahams and Gay continue with an example. To illustrate my point about female teachers, I have replaced "brother" in "Right on, brother" with "teacher" in the student's dialogue.

> On this particular day, the students have decided not to do anything in class. The teacher enters and instructs the students to begin work. No one says or does anything. Then one student begins to sing softly to himself. The teacher asks the singer to be quiet and return to his regularly assigned seat. The student responds with "Right on, [teacher], I'm gonna move," and he does. The teacher says something else and the student answers, "Right on, [teacher]." The teacher, very much irritated says "Shut up." The student answers very softly, "Right on, [teacher]." The teacher says, "I don't like your attitude today and if you don't be quiet I'm gonna put you out." The student, more forceful this time says "Right on, [teacher]." The teacher answers with "Get out," and the student responds, "Right on [teacher]," as he slowly walks out of the door (p. 165).

Even though this woofin' episode was written in 1975, the same "game" is "being run" on teachers today. The teacher was perceived as incompetent, out of control, so the student won that game. The students in that class have lost respect for the teacher, confirming their supposition that she is a pushover. Now, they can run that same game on her again whenever they decide to do so.

Foster (1986), who has conducted considerable research on teachers' handling of this verbal strategy, might recommend that the teacher reproduce a supply of "woof tickets" to hand out to that student as a surprise. This effort might acknowledge the student's adeptness and confirm the teacher's understanding and appreciation of his attempt to "run a game" on her. She could hand out the ticket, quickly lead the class back to learning tasks at hand and still maintain control over the situation without antagonizing.

Here is another woofin' scenario that Foster describes as "Reality 58". It could also be called a "Showdown".

> A new teacher was walking in the hall when a few boys approached him from the opposite direction. One of the boys peeled off from the group, and as he and the teacher came face to face, he moved his hand out in front of the

teacher, placed his palm against the wall, and looked at the teacher (pg. 194).

What would you do if a student "laid that silent rap" on you? What are the options?

1. You could stop, turn the other way and run. If you flee, the student has won. He loses respect for you and will not listen to another thing you say. He sold the woof ticket and you bought it.

2. You could become visibly upset and lecture to the student about the value of respect, telling him you will report him to the office if he doesn't move. The student as in the previous scenario would probably show no visible response, ignore you and/or aggravate you even more. He might even push you into hitting him by simply out-staring you or laughing or sneering in your face. If you hit him, you have lost again. He'll probably hit you back. Remember, he's selling tickets in front of an audience and they will encourage him. No one wants to lose face.

3. You could sell some woof tickets of your own. You could out-stare him with a look that is "badder" than his and say emphatically "Move!" Or, you could quickly snap his arm at the pressure point, and move him out of the way. You win his respect by not yielding to his efforts to frighten you. Any time you touch a student you take a chance, for a lawsuit though, so weigh this decision.

4. Foster's suggestion of "wolf tickets" to hand out to successful woofers might work here. This might disarm the student. Remember, the objective of woofin' is to avoid physical confrontation through effective intimidation.

5. You might divert the student's attention by asking him a question that requires him to explain something to you. This tactic could cause him to move his hand from the wall and use it to make gestures as he is giving an explanation. As you follow through with the explanation, you could move forward past the student and his friends.

6. Or, you could observe how an African American teacher who understands the strategies reacts with his/her students in a similar situation. Remember, in the Black community respect is earned, not given automatically with a title or a position. Many African Ameri-

can students will be skeptical initially of your intentions. Through being consistent and fair in your interactions with them, you will be able to establish a good rapport.

Kochman (1981) found that verbally aggressive behavior is regarded very differently in Black and White communities. As with woofin', African Americans hold that angry verbal disputes *do not* have to escalate to actual physical fighting. "... Insults and threats can be maintained by Blacks at the verbal level *without* violence necessarily resulting." Whereas, "... Whites view it as a clear warning of *intent to act upon that threat*" (pp. 48-49). So, from a White cultural perspective, woofin' is regarded as a prelude to a fight, not as an attempt *to avoid* a fight which is the actual intent of this verbal strategy.

It is quite possible, then for White and/or insensitive teachers to report woofin' to the office, and label frequent woofers as "overly aggressive" and "a discipline problem." An African American male who continually exercises his adeptness at woofin' could be placed on in-house suspension or in programs for the "behaviorally disordered," responses that are inappropriate for this verbal strategy.

In an interesting account Smith describes his personal experiences as a "disruptive male" who became adept at the verbal strategies and was subsequently penalized educationally and socially (1974, pp. 1-14).

Other cultures also revere verbal facility and use similar strategies. During the 1990-91 war in the Middle East, Saudi and Iraqi foes used television to vent their anger in rhymed verse in an ancient pre-Islamic custom that still remains in the educational curriculum and is studied by youngsters.

> ... warfare has actually been averted when antagonists have vented their aggression in verse (Ehud Ya'ari, p. 26).

Playin' the Dozens

Playing the dozens, which may begin as early as age eight, is considered a manhood rite (Abrahams (1963), Smith (1974), Schultz (1977), Hannerz (1977), Nobles (1980), Cooke (1980), and Kunjufu (1986, 1988). Schulz (1977) reports that boys begin to play the Dozens at about eleven years of age. Although girls begin the game at about 11 1/2 years, it still usually carries an assertion of masculinity. (Boys as young as six play the game!)

Smitherman (1977) considers playing the Dozens a form of signification, a discourse mode. Signification is a culturally acceptable way to talk openly about someone. In playing the Dozens, two opponents dual verbally, making derogatory remarks about each others' family members, usually the mother. The basis for this game is call-response, discussed previously in this chapter. Each player is appreciated and judged by the group, whose responsibility is also to urge the players on. The rules include avoidance of talk about a deceased family member, never playing the game with a stranger, and using "inaccurate" statements of reality to defame one another's mother for fear that a fight might ensue, which sometimes happens when opponents hit a sensitive nerve (Kunjufu, 1986, pp. 16-17).

The winner of the game is determined by the audience, who judges both players' reactions to one another's comments. The cultural hero is the player who hurls the most linguistically-derogatory comments and still maintains his composure.

The slurs can be in the form of a rhyme:

> I saw yo momma on the railroad track, looked at her and said, "Oooh, git back." (Kunjufu, 1988, p. 16).

Or, the slur can just be the words "yo momma." When I was in school, girls and boys played the game. In order to keep the teacher from knowing what we were doing, we just cleared our throats and that meant "your mother" (yo momma). We would play the game openly on the school bus and in the hallways.

Smitherman (1977) claims that the original verses of the Dozens included twelve sex acts, each one given in words that rhymed with the numbers from 1 to 12. Abrahams (1976) says that references to sex acts are what distinguish the Dirty Dozens from the Dozens. For an in-depth discussion, see Labov (1972), who has grouped examples of rhymes into categories of complex syntactic structures which have strict discourse rules.

There is ample evidence that the origins of this game are in Africa. Hare and Hare (1985) report that playing the Dozens might be a re-creation of a Nigerian ritual function called *trickstering* during which the boy puts down the father verbally. Abrahams (1976) contends that the intense devotion an African boy has for his mother causes fights when another says disparaging remarks about her. Nobles (1980) in his treatise on African Philosophy reveals that traditions were handed down from father to son. He describes ritualized orations and dance ceremonies that were used to release suppressed emotions.

> ...slavery unknowingly permitted the cultural trans-mission of the African traditional emphasis or oration and its consequent effects on the mind or memory to remain pretty much in tact. White... suggests that playing the "dozens" as part of the oral tradition is a game used by black youngsters to teach themselves to keep cool, think fast under pressure, and not say what is really on their minds. Things like rapping and the dozens could also be viewed as initiation rites or possibly instances where the "power" of the word is used to make the "individual" psychologically feel better (p. 34).

Foster (1986) reports on African origins. Several are among the Ashanti natives, who sang Opo verses and were known for verbal and nonverbal insults about ancestors. There are also references to the Trinidadian game Mamaguy, the African Giguku's taboo that infuri-ates a man to mention his mother's name in an indecent way. The Dahomean game involves a joking relationship and African songs of recrimination.

It is interesting to note historical accounts of cultures that used ritual insults to precede a battle or even to avoid it. In the *Holy Bible,* Samuel 17:43-46 during which David slays Goliath, a similar dialogue ensues as the two warriors hurl verbal insults preceding combat:

> And the Philistine said to David, Come to me, and I will give thy flesh unto the fowls of the air, and to the beasts of the field.
> Then said David to the Philistine, Thou comest to me with a sword, and with a spear, and with a shield: but I come to thee in the name of the Lord of hosts, the God of the armies of Israel, whom thou has defied.
> This day will the Lord deliver thee unto mine hand:

and I will smite thee, and take thine head from thee; and I will give the carcasses of the host of the Philistines this day unto the fowls of the air, and to the wild beast of the earth; that all the earth may know that there is a God in Israel.

The events in this book are dated to the closing century of the second millennium B.C. During the 1990-91 war in the Middle East, an ancient Semitic tradition was revived when Saudi television aired ritual insults in rhyme written by Saudi poets. The Iraqi army retorted with poets who could quote from ancient verse in the verbal war that preceded the physical war.

...And given the possibility that the trading of gibes could turn out to be the full extent of the war, the question of who is better at it takes on considerable importance. Whose barbs have been more devastating? Whose poets have produced more quotable quotes? These questions occupy Arab viewers almost as much as the issue of who enjoys better odds on the battlefield, and few will deny that the Saudis are winning the verbal war hands down (Ehud Ya'ari and Ina Friedman, p. 26).

Foster also includes a description of how the game was used during slavery. Here is an excerpt from *OSSIE: The Autobiography of a Black Woman.*

It was a game slaves used to play, only they weren't just playing for fun. They was playing to teach themselves and their sons how to stay alive. The whole idea was to learn to take whatever the master said to you without answering back or hitting him, 'cause that was the way a slave had to be, so's he could go on living. It maybe was a bad game, but it was necessary (pp. 228-229).

Other names for the dozens include lists offered by Abrahams (1976), Smith (1974), Foster (1986), and numerous other men and boys I have interviewed: checkin', crackin', getting down on the crib, getting on the kitchen folks, getting on moms, going to the kitchen, giving a man the spoke, joaning (jonin), playing, putting a man on the wheel, signifying (siggin'), and sounding. Although names vary from city to city and region to region, every male I have consulted, from school superintendents and college presidents to cab drivers and school students - all know about the dozens and/or admit they have played the game. Most have related a specific humorous incident that stood out in their minds. Some have stated outright "I don't play that game any more" or "that's a dangerous game."

Smitherman describes the game as "... a competitive oral test of linguistic ingenuity and verbal fluency" (p.131). Hannerz (1977) reports that joke telling usually accompanies "joning," as the game is called in Washington, D.C. He claims that the slurs most often condemn the mother for some kind of moral or sexual deviation - an extreme departure from her idealized role as a feminine woman. Kunjufu (1988) summarizes the five competencies of a good dozens player:

1. He must control his emotions. Here, in the presence of friends, terribly derogatory statements are made about his mother, who is dear to him.
2. He must begin to search for his masculine identity as he pulls away from the strong influence of his mother by withstanding derogatory comments.
3. He must develop the ability to make words rhyme and utter them spontaneously.
4. He must be able to think on his feet and counter with an even more clever slur upon his opponent's female relative.
5. He must be brave enough to take the risk of being "bested" in front of his peers. Losing means disapproval, being proved ineffective at words, and that is connected to being effeminate in the eyes of peers (Abrahams, 1963, p. 55; Kunjufu, 1986, p. 17).

Here is a typical example of how playing the Dozens can disrupt the classroom:

The students in your science class are about to do an experiment. All materials have been distributed. You have explained the details for each group. One student loudly accuses the other in his group of talking about his momma. The students face each other as if they *might* begin to fight.

How would you respond in this situation? Here are some options:

1. Direct the other groups to begin their work. Go to the two players and state clearly that you do not allow the game of the Dozens (use the appropriate name for your locale) in your room. This tells the students you are aware of the game. You understand what they are doing, but will not permit students to play it in your room.

2. Stop the class and talk briefly about the game. An integral part of the game is that the players must be convincing. Students can appear angry at one another as they shout slurs. Five minutes later they are still friends. Most games can be diffused by simply announcing that the game is over. Be convincing and be consistent if this should happen again.

3. Tell the other students to begin their experiments. Mediate for the two players. "Just because he talked about your mother, it doesn't mean what he said is true. Now let's move on to the experiment at hand." This game might have started a day earlier or on the school bus and have been continued throughout the halls prior to the class meeting.

4. Diffuse the game and move the class to completing the experiment. Set aside a specific time to talk to the class about the game. Be certain that students learn about the history and the purpose of the game. It is designed to let off steam and relieve tension. It is a manhood rite developed to teach the players how to be strong in the face of danger or in fearful situations and think on their feet. Mention Kunjufu's competencies and turn those competencies into advantages by having students match wits about some character in a history lesson or the concepts involved in a science lesson. They should be permitted to speak from notes they have taken. Classmates could award points for accuracy and delivery.

5. Set up debates on the content of topics discussed in your class. Debate on current topics such as abortion, teen pregnancy, drugs, AIDS, premarital sex, etc. Be certain to channel your best Dozens players into leading roles in this debate.

6. It would be unwise to place a lot of focus on the fact that the boys may come to blows. This detracts from

instructional time and rewards undesirable behavior. Hill (1989) recommends that teachers locate a mentor - another teacher in the same school who is adept at handling boys' use of verbal strategies-and talk with your mentor about how to handle these efforts at self identity.

In the classroom, peers playing the Dozens can present a serious problem for the teacher. Especially if he or she is unaware of the game and its significance.

Teachers must encourage and provide opportunities for students to read and learn more about African and African American history. Use the Appendix of this book to locate resources and references that might be helpful. Consult Smith's (1974) *Ebonics Questionnaire and Glossary of Oral Expressive Styles* (pp. 156-185). Show the list to your principal and your librarian so that these materials will become an integral part of your school's library collection.

A Serious Dilemma

In many educational settings, it is Black males who are most frequently placed in the corner in classrooms, sent to the principal's office, suspended, and expelled. The negative statistics mentioned at the beginning of this chapter help to create low expectations, college textbooks and college professors describe "the numerous problems" of Black people. Indeed, Dent (1989) contends that these negative images of Black males are an integral part of the educational system, and they are a primary cause of student failure because they foster low expectations on the part of the teacher.

Kunjufu (1988) has provided thorough coverage of the dilemma Black males face as they use these verbal strategies in the schools. He reports that playing the Dozens has caused far too many Black males to be placed in corners, sent to the principal's office, removed by suspension or expulsion, or pushed into remedial and special education programs. Students recognize that this happens, so they devise strategies for survival - verbal strategies they can use to maintain some measure of control over the school situation where all the cards seem to be stacked against them. They develop their verbal techniques using those same skills that help them survive in their communities or on the streets.

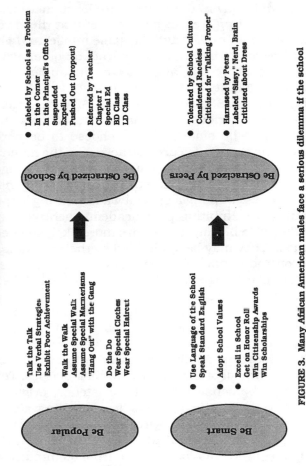

A Dilemma for Some Young African American Males

Be Popular

- Talk the Talk
  Use Verbal Strategies
  Exhibit Poor Achievement
- Walk the Walk
  Assume Special Walk
  Assume Special Mannerisms
  "Hang Out" with the Gang
- Do the Do
  Wear Special Clothes
  Wear Special Haircut

Be Ostracized by School

- Labeled by School as a Problem
  In the Corner
  In the Principal's Office
  Suspended
  Expelled
  Pushed Out (Dropout)
- Referred by Teacher
  Chapter I
  Special Ed
  BD Class
  LD Class

Be Smart

- Use Language of the School
  Speak Standard English
- Adopt School Values
- Excell in School
  Get on Honor Roll
  Win Citizenship Awards
  Win Scholarships

Be Ostracized by Peers

- Tolerated by School Culture
  Considered Raceless
  Criticized for "Talking Proper"
- Harrassed by Peers
  Labeled "Sissy," Nerd, Brain
  Criticized about Dress

© EAB Dandy 1991

FIGURE 3. Many African American males face a serious dilemma if the school forces them to choose between being popular and being smart.

It is indeed unfortunate that, for the most part, those African American males who are most adept at rappin', woofin', and playin' the Dozens are least successful in the school setting. Yet, to be successful at these verbal games students must have the same intellectual ability that is needed to become school leaders: quick wit and ability to capture the attention of an audience with linguistic ingenuity and verbal fluency.

Kunjufu (1988) contends that African American males face a serious dilemma in the schools; to be popular or to be smart. If they choose to be popular among their peers, they are ostracized by the macroculture of the school. Being popular entails practicing and perfecting stylized verbal strategies, wearing name-brand clothes, walking a special walk, wearing a special haircut, and exhibiting poor academic achievement. If they choose to be smart, they are more likely to succeed in school. They may be applauded by their teachers and listed on the honor roll. They may become *bidialectal*, using standard English in the classroom and BC distinctive features when in the company of their peer group. The choice of being smart means ostracism by the African American peer group and being labeled a nerd, a brainiac, or a sissy.

It is the responsibility of teachers to learn to communicate with all of the children in their classes. Teachers should be sensitized to the existence, origin, and intent of verbal strategies. Teachers need to watch and listen for them in their classrooms and search for more effective ways to communicate with those who use them. Discipline problems may stem from communicative issues and conflicts between cultures.

African American males who appear to challenge the teacher's authority may be selling woof tickets. Those who are not listening quietly when the teacher is presenting a lesson may be giving the teacher feedback on the information presented. Those who interrupt another student may be responding to a call that has been issued. Those who are socializing and responding in a loud voice may be searching for their identity, asserting their masculinity, and confirming friendships. Those who *seem* to be using physical means to settle a conflict may be making their best effort to *avoid* a fight. Students who are successful at these verbal strategies must have the same intellectual ability that is needed to become school leaders.

The way you handle incidents such as these will be determined by the rapport you have established with your class and whether or not you have made a serious effort to understand this natural process of moving from boyhood to manhood. Continue to *listen to your students* as they confirm their attempts at self-identity. Be consistent in your treatment of them. Students will always test you, but it is your responsibility to control the teaching/learning situation. Consistently low levels of academic performance for one culture must be viewed as unacceptable.

Culturally-sensitive teachers take time daily to read aloud to their students.

CHAPTER SIX

DEVELOPING COMMUNICATIVE COMPETENCE

Everything that occurs within a school, and especially in the classroom, involves *communication*, the act of sharing information. Communication is the medium of instruction, assessment, interpersonal relationships, group interactions, parent/community relations, and counseling. Most behavior problems, and their resolutions, involve communication issues. In sum, communication permeates education (Orlando Taylor, 1987, p. 1).

Taylor defines communication as the act of sharing information. Effective communication must include a sender as well as a receiver. Learning is largely dependent upon some form of communication: listening, speaking, reading and/or writing. Language is the primary medium that is used for communication. It is the responsibility of the school to build student's ability to use language. Students must learn the rules of language such as subject-verb agreement, plural formation and the different ways of showing ownership, as well as how they can *use* the language to perform such tasks as introducing oneself, requesting information, and ending a conversation. They should learn how to use the language appropriately in a variety of situations depending upon the audience, the topic, and the speaker's purpose. They must learn how to communicate in their home language as well as in the language of the school, the standard language, standard English.

Different cultures generally have their own rules and ways of using language. Cross-cultural miscommunication can occur between two individuals whose cultures have different rules for interacting or sending and receiving information (Taylor, 1987).

You read in the chapter on African origins and verbal strategies, that verbal ability is prized in the African American community. As early as age five, boys learn to become adept at using words to convince, persuade, or impress. This use of language becomes a practice that enables a young male to pass from boyhood to manhood. Verbal strategies are imitated, encouraged, practiced, and perfected.

Schools that are unaware of the use of verbal strategies, often develop policies that punish students who use the strategies. Here is a true story that illustrates my point. In this situation, Lamar used a verbal strategy to convince one of his classmates to leave him alone. Indeed, his dialectal communicative competence is misinterpreted by his teacher, the counselor and the school's administrative policies.

And the Cycle Begins....

The narrator regularly visits elementary schools to observe practicum students who are enrolled in pre-service education courses. As the narrator walks around the school she passes an African American male who is being punished and is seated on a chair just outside the principal's office. The following dialogue took place in early October, one month into the new school year. The narrator asks the name of the student and the teacher's name and his grade. The student replies...

Student: Lamar. Mrs. O'Keefe room, I'm in first grade.
Narrator: Why are you sitting in the office?
Lamar: The teacher put me out.
Narrator: Why?
Lamar: Cause I told Betsy I was going to bash her face in.
Narrator: Why did you say that?
Lamar: She keep on messin' wif me.

Narrator: Tell me exactly what she did.

Lamar: She tease me, say I'm dumb and bad and be having to go to the office.

Narrator: Were you going to bash her face in?

Lamar: No. My momma say I'm not suppose to fight.

(Just then the counselor approached and joined in the conversation.)

Counselor: Lamar's mother hasn't contacted the school, so he must remain in the principal's office until she does. (The mother lives in an inner-city pocket about 15 miles from the school.)

Narrator: How long has he been in the office?

Counselor: This is the third day. Lamar, did you give your mother the note I wrote to her?

Lamar: Yes ma'am.

Counselor: Well, is she going to call me or come to the school? You know the rule is that you may not go back to your classroom until she calls and talks to me about your behavior. Did she say anything to you about the note?

Lamar: She say I know I'm not suppose to fight.

Narrator: Lamar, did you hit Betsy?

Lamar: No ma'am.

Counselor: Well, Mrs. O'Keefe said you were very mean to Betsy and you threatened her.

Narrator: Was Betsy punished for teasing Lamar?

Counselor: I don't believe she was. You know, Lamar has a history of fighting. This is his third time in the office since school started.

And so the cycle begins...

After having read Chapter Five, you should have identified the verbal strategy used by Lamar as woofin', the strategy designed to *avoid* a fight.

If Lamar had really intended to hit Betsy, he would have done so earlier. Instead, he used communicative competence in BC to frighten Betsy so that she would stop teasing him and leave him alone. Mrs. O'Keefe interpreted Lamar's wolfing as an *intent* to fight. The school's discipline policy clearly specifies that fighting is against the rules. Mrs. O'Keefe was insensitive to the real meaning in Lamar's words. Instead of sending Lamar to the office, Mrs. O'Keefe should have told Lamar to resume his work and continued teaching. Betsy, who never

1st GRADE

	BLACK		WHITE		TOTAL
	MALE	FEMALE	MALE	FEMALE	
TOTAL ENROLLMENT	1,037	927	849	788	3,601
PERCENTAGE	28.2%	25.2%	23.1%	21.4%	
NO. OUT OF SCHOOL SUSPENSION	95	15	17	0	127
NO. RETAINED	73	44	38	15	170
READING MEAN	43.5%	47.6%	53.8%	56.6%	*
MATH MEAN	46.4%	49.5%	60.4%	59.6%	*

* In reading Black Males begin in 1st grade at 10.3 percentage points below White Males.

* In math Black Males begin in 1st grade at 14.0 percentage points below White Males.

SOURCE: Chatham-Savannah Youth Futures Authority, Feb.'91

was punished for teasing Lamar, knew just what to do to get him into trouble with the teacher.

The school has also established a policy that penalizes working parents who live a distance from the school. The mother, who did not have a car, had to take off from her job to come to the school. More seriously, Lamar's education was placed on "hold" until his mother could come to the school. This is how a child whose behavior does not fit the cultural norm can be pushed out of the classroom. In the second month of a new school year, Lamar, a first grader, has already missed nine days of classes. The counselor has concluded that Lamar has "developed a reputation" from the three other times he had been sent to the office.

In all of those instances Lamar was excluded from the learning environment. Lamar's stay in the office was making him miss instruction; miss out on the early establishment of classroom routines, miss out on early attempts teachers generally use at the beginning of the year to acclimate children to the school environment and let them know what is expected of them.

Mrs. O'Keefe, the counselor, and the principal were insensitive to the fact that other cultures can engage in verbal confrontation and continue to maintain communication without it escalating into a fight. This cultural difference led to a communication problem—a miscommunication. Instead of talking to Lamar about the situation, Mrs. O'Keefe pushed him out of the classroom. (This same "push your 'problems' away" mindset occurs in the larger society as vast numbers of African American males are sent to jail.)

Another Serious Dilemma

Just as you read in Chapter Five about the predicament facing many young African American males, there is another very serious dilemma facing teachers. Teachers, regardless of their race, are often forced to choose between the values and cultural conventions of the school and those of the non-dominant culture, which is often the majority of the students who are having problems in the school. Whatever path they choose, teachers face a dilemma.

The macroculture of most public schools in this

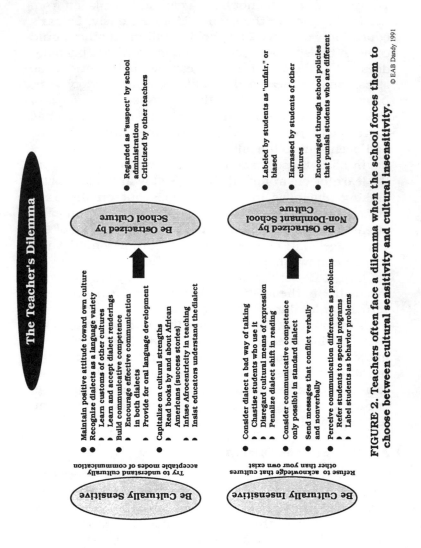

The Teacher's Dilemma

Be Culturally Sensitive
Try to understand culturally acceptable modes of communication

- Maintain positive attitude toward own culture
- Recognize dialects as a language variety
  - Learn customs of other cultures
  - Learn and accept dialect renderings
- Build communicative competence
  - Encourage effective communication in both dialects
  - Provide for oral language development
- Capitalize on cultural strengths
  - Read books by and about African Americans (success stories)
  - Infuse Afrocentricity in teaching
  - Insist educators understand the dialect

Be Ostracized by School Culture

- Regarded as "suspect" by school administration
- Criticized by other teachers

Be Culturally Insensitive
Refuse to acknowledge that cultures other than your own exist

- Consider dialect a bad way of talking
  - Chastise students who use it
  - Disregard cultural means of expression
  - Penalize dialect shift in reading
- Consider communicative competence only possible in standard dialect
  - Send messages that conflict verbally and nonverbally
- Perceive communication differences as problems
  - Refer students to special programs
  - Label students as behavior problems

Be Ostracized by Non-Dominant School Culture

- Labeled by students as "unfair," or biased
- Harrassed by students of other cultures
- Encouraged through school policies that punish students who are different

© E.A.B. Dandy 1991

FIGURE 2. Teachers often face a dilemma when the school forces them to choose between cultural sensitivity and cultural insensitivity.

country today is European American—the vast majority of administrators and teachers are European American (Chira, 1989). They usually set the rules and decide what constitutes an infringement of the rules. As they develop the rules, the school administration and teachers are culturally insensitive if they do not acknowledge that cultures other than their own exist. Since they are all thinking from the same cultural point of view, they are largely unaware of conflicting communicative patterns used by other cultures. Anything that is different is perceived as negative or bad. So, efforts to communicate that are foreign to the rule-setters and are considered unacceptable, and students who use them are often subsequently labeled as "behavior problems."

Taylor (1990, p. 33) includes the following categories of communicative behaviors which are usually considered unacceptable in most school environments, but constitute culturally different ways of using the language:

1. Challenging the teacher's authority
2. Using obscene language in class
3. Not listening quietly when the teacher is presenting a lesson
4. Moving around the room when the teacher is presenting a lesson
5. Interrupting another student
6. Not waiting until one person has finished speaking before taking a turn
7. Responding in a loud voice
8. Not walking away during discord
9. Using physical means to settle a conflict
10. Showing emotion during discord

Culturally-insensitive teachers consider dialect as a bad way of talking. They chastise students when they use the dialect and disregard cultural verbal and non-verbal modes of expression. During oral reading, these insensitive teachers label any dialect rendering as totally incorrect. They contend that communicative competence is only possible in the standard dialect - which they often perceive as their own dialect. These teachers may say that they want all students to succeed, but their nonverbal messages (such as the number of times they call on students, what they say when students answer, their lack of eye contact, etc.) communicate that they do not believe these children will succeed.

These teachers systematically exclude culturally different students from the learning environment. Insensitive teachers tell students through their actions that they are inferior. Culturally-insensitive teachers are quick to send students to the office and refer them to special programs, such as in Chapter One, and classes for the mentally retarded. To them, discipline constitutes punishment - something harsh is usually done to students to serve as a deterrent to further misbehavior: students are denied privileges, isolated from the group, and isolated from the classroom.

Culturally-insensitive teachers often operate on the "blame the victim" premise: "Since this student does not respond to any of my (limited) repertoire of strategies for classroom management, something must be wrong with this student. So, I need to remove the student from my room. He/She probably has a learning disability, or is retarded, so I'll *refer* him/her to a special program for the behaviorally disordered or learning disabled." They view discipline as a penalty rather than a way of helping students gain self-control.

I remember so clearly observing in the classroom of a kindergarten teacher who placed one African American male on the periphery of the classroom with the front of his desk touching the wall. I asked her if this was a permanent location for the child, and her answer was, "yes." When I told her she was excluding this child from the learning environment, she replied, "But you don't understand. This boy *cannot* work in group situations."

This kindergartener will never learn how to work in that group if the teacher never affords him the opportunity to do so. If you want to teach a child how to eat in a restaurant, you don't keep her away from the restaurant. You talk with her about the kinds of things she will do there, about the topics she can discuss, what she should wear and you *take* her there and *show* her what to do, what to say, and how to act, and when she comes home, you talk to her some more. And, then you take her back to the restaurant again and again, each time rewarding her successive approximations to the behavior you desire. Permanently excluding her from the place you want her to go will *never* teach her how to act in that place.

Culturally-insensitive teachers can be Black or White. If they are African American, they may have been led along with the rest of American society, to believe they should shun any language or customs even remotely related to "the ghetto." Culturally-insensitive teachers have been led to believe that anything connected to being Black is a social stigma. They may have spent a significant amount of time trying to get out of the ghetto, and any reminders of their lives there are considered insulting.

Insensitive African American teachers often treat Black children *worse* than their insensitive White counterparts. They embarrass or humiliate Black children, talk openly about them in the teacher's lounge and generally hold lower expectations for their Black students. When the students do not perform well, they feel justified in giving them lower grades.

In fact, insensitive teachers determine grades on the bases of language and behavior rather than achievement. These reactions on the part of the culturally insensitive teachers are often encouraged or condoned by administrators, who do not question consistently low attendance and achievement by African American students. Principals permit teachers, often the same culturally-insensitive ones, to send large numbers of Black children to the office and treat cultural differences as behavioral problems. They suspend Black children, expel them, refer them to programs for the mentally retarded, learning disabled and/or language disordered, and generally blame them for their inadequacies.

These insensitive teachers are encouraged by administrators who designate them as "master teachers", "grade level chairpersons", or "student teaching supervisors".

One trait that researchers often attribute to African Americans is that they tend to have a keen sense of fairness, they are quick to analyze and perceive injustice and are sensitive to nonverbal cues (Hilliard and Akbar as reported by Hale-Benson, 1986, pp. 42-43). When students perceive that a given teacher is insensitive or unfair, they make life miserable for the teacher by harassing him/her, acting out in class, talking to other students about that teacher or *openly* engaging in any of the ten behaviors listed by Taylor earlier in this chapter.

On the other hand, culturally-sensitive teachers seek to understand culturally acceptable modes of communication other than their own. These teachers maintain positive attitudes toward their own culture. They recognize that dialects are a variety of language and they allow students to use dialects in their classroom. The goal of these teachers is to build communicative competence in the standard dialect without degrading the dialect of the students. Culturally-sensitive teachers openly teach students to distinguish between dialect renderings and Standard English (SE). Since these teachers are familiar with most of BC's distinctive features, they can demonstrate to students what they are doing with the language when they speak in their own dialect. These teachers provide ample opportunities for students to communicate in speaking and writing with one another. They set up role-playing situations wherein students have to select the most appropriate language for the situation or audience: formal or informal language, school talk, home talk, or street talk. (See Chapter Seven for activities.) These teachers provide problem-solving situations in which students must *talk through* how they would react to peer pressure to do drugs or cheat on a test or any number of appropriate situations. They allow students time to learn from one another by using cooperative learning (that will be discussed later in this chapter). These culturally-sensitive teachers learn to capitalize on cultural strengths.

Now, both Black and White teachers can be culturally sensitive, and since the vast majority of teachers in the dawn of the 21st century will be White, more White teachers *need* to join the ranks of the culturally sensitive. They find and share techniques for capitalizing on cultural strengths through developing the competencies involved in everyday popular verbal strategies and call-response. They "infuse the curriculum with an orientation that reflects the heritage of people of African descent" (Jenifer, 1990) by teaching about the contributions African Americans made to science, math, language arts, history and other content areas. Culturally-sensitive teachers search for connections between language systems by studying the culture and language and by infusing the concept of Africentricity into the schools.

Culturally-sensitive teachers work with librarians to provide book titles about African Americans for teachers to read and to refer their students. (See Appendix.) They take time daily to read aloud to their students, regardless of the grade level they are teaching.

As they seek better educational credentials and attend graduate school, culturally-sensitive teachers urge teacher training institutions to also provide exposure for preservice teachers in classrooms that have other culturally sensitive teachers who are successful with African American students. They share books such as Janice Hale-Benson's text that describes learning styles of Black children and Mary Rhodes Hoover's text that describes successful schools for Black children. They also seek awareness of the African American culture by reading books from Kunjufu's series (*Countering the Conspiracy*, volumes 1, 2, and 3) that enlighten the reader about the societal pressures on African American males.

Culturally-sensitive teachers communicate with the parents. They go out of their way to make personal contacts with them and tell parents positive things their children are doing. They consistently hold high expectations for their students and see that the students meet them. They take seriously the study of the language/dialect and recognize the need for students to develop competence in their own dialect as well as the dialect of the school. They prepare their children to deal with the realities of bias and racism as they apply the use of language in daily situations. They teach their students to use language in a variety of settings and contexts and demonstrate the value in learning the languages of culture and of power.

As they teach these concepts to their students, these culturally-sensitive teachers run the risk of being ostracized by the school. Often times they are labeled as "racists" if they are African American and "nigger lovers" if they are European American. They are hassled by administrators for being "aggressive" and "militant", when in essence they are only being assertive and proud of their race and culture. They are labeled "trouble makers" and "social problem solvers" who are extending beyond teaching the curriculum.

Historically, sensitivity to other cultures has not been advocated by the vast majority of the public schools in this country. As stated in Chapter One, the macroculture of public schools often forces those who attend to abandon their culture and blend into the culture in power. Students who are different from the majority school population are oftentimes considered bad or inferior, and anything related to their culture is put down or denigrated.

Those teachers who advocate any culture/language/dialect other than what is emphasized by the macroculture are ostracized by their peers and the school administration. Indeed, teachers who go out of their way to be sensitive to the needs of poor children (many times, new teachers) are teased and taunted by their peers with statements such as "I don't know why you're wasting your time with him. What do you expect he'll amount to? Look where he came from. I had his sister last year - the whole family is like that." Or, those teachers who are envious taunt with "What are you trying to do, make it hard for us? You can work yourself to death if you want to. I was like you when I first came here - tried to change the world, but I soon learned not to go out of my way for those children. You don't get paid for that. Those kids don't appreciate anything you try to do for them."

The majority of teachers teaching African American children today are culturally insensitive. Their teacher training institutions offer *no* courses in cultural sensitivity or classroom management. Since the students they teach do not communicate in the same ways teachers do, they label the children "nonverbal", "culturally deprived" and "disadvantaged". The latter two labels, still used today, are remnants of the 60s and the language deficit theory. (See Chapter Two.)

Unfortunately, the American media has painted a very negative picture of African Americans - especially males. As you saw in Chapters Four and Five, the negative treatment of African American males began in Africa when foreign invaders penetrated the land through a series of wars. When enslaved Africans were brought to this country, the denigration continued. They were traded and sold like cattle. This denigration has been perpetuated by legislative bodies who cut federally sponsored programs for the poor. George Bush's 1989 presidential campaign and the use of Willie Horton as the person Michael Dukakis supposedly let out of jail made it acceptable in American to hate the negative image of the African American male. Obvious leaders of the Ku Klux Klan, like David Duke, can run for public offices in Louisiana and receive 44% of the vote. Racism on college campuses has been the subject of numerous television documentaries.

Stover's (1990, p. 14) article entitled "The New Racism" avows "...Racism is alive and well in the public schools... Across the U.S., schools are experiencing a disturbing increase in incidents of racism and prejudice, ranging from exchanges of racial epithets to violence along racial lines." The racism prevalent in the larger society has spread to the schools. Flashed on the news worldwide was the home video exposure of the brutal beating of Los Angeles citizen Rodney King by many police officers and refusal of Police Chief Daryl Gates to resign. Two weeks prior to the incident, the President of the United States had commended Gates and the LA Police Department for their "outstanding leadership." The failure of the system to really punish this police chief and the officers sends a signal to the American public that brutality is acceptable.

This mentality has spread to the school setting. And schools across the country are engaged in a massive "push out" of African American and Hispanic American students whose culture and cultural expectations are vastly different from the macroculture of the school. The scenario entitled "And So The Cycle Begins" at the beginning of this chapter is an excellent example of how the "push out" often begins.

Establishing Awareness

How can teachers escape or work out of this serious dilemma? It must begin with awareness - awareness on the part of everyone in the school that other, legitimate cultures/languages/dialects exist and are effective in communicating. Someone, perhaps an outside consultant, can conduct a series of workshops that describe dialects, in general, and make teachers aware that everyone speaks a dialect, even the teachers themselves. Teachers need to first study the features of their dialect and then relate their dialect to Black Communications so that they can see the similarities and actually discern how the dialects differ in sounds, syllables, words, word order, and modes of communication. They could engage in many of the activities provided in Chapter Seven of this text.

Basically, teachers have to regard dialect different speakers as human beings who *are developing* the ability to communicate in two different modes: Standard or Educated English and Black Communications. They must recognize that language is a medium of exchange. In short, they must teach students to become bidialectal and be able to switch from one code to another whenever and wherever the need arises. They must learn that the use of the standard language can serve as a passport, allowing them to travel anywhere they want to go (Brice-Finch, 1991). It enables them to communicate in most educated circles around the world. Teachers must recognize that *they* were not born speaking Standard English as adults. Just as someone taught them the language, teachers must teach the language to the children. The key lies in the teacher's *attitude* and *expectations* for dialect speakers as they build communicative competence.

> ...An alarming percentage of students who speak nonstandard English are failing to acquire standard English, the language of Education. Moreover, many students who acquire standard English, do so while being taught to reject the language of their home, community and peers. In the process, they are robbed of an effective element of social solidarity, which is an important element of the cultural heritage (Orlando Taylor, 1987, p. 19).

Afrocentricity

Afrocentricity is a term used by African American scholars to describe the African-centered view as it can be applied to education. This view of education capitalizes on the strengths of the African and African American culture, *without* denigrating any other culture. It emphasizes the study of African history as well as African American history and reveals the contributions made by people of that culture to the history of the world in virtually every subject area - from art to science. Franklyn Jenifer, President of Howard University, and Abena Walker, a Teaching Methodology Specialist have discussed their views in articles appearing in the *Washington Post*. Portions of these articles have been reprinted below with permission.

According to Abena Walker, there are definite benefits to infusing Afrocentricity into the schools.

Afrocentric Education
Would Benefit All

Opponents of Afrocentric education are getting venomous. It attacks Europeans and Western civilization, they say. It is false history, replete with improbable assertions, they contend. "Militant" and "angry" black scholars are pictured as arrayed against white scholars who are too afraid of being called "racists" to denounce them.

While admitting that the history of Africa and black contributions have been omitted or played down dramatically, the people wary of Afrocentric education balk at proposed remedies.

It is understandable that challenges to the European-centered curriculum engender alarm in establishment circles, but an Afrocentric curriculum is not an attempt to destroy Western content. It is an attempt to correct and balance history.

The educational underachievement of many inner-city children, in particular, is well known. In the District, nearly half the students drop out before receiving a high school diploma. African American parents have complained, meanwhile, that their children were given an inaccurate and distorted view of history in their books and classrooms, prompting them to applaud the contributions of other cultures and denigrate their own. Much of today's controversy centers on whether Afrocentric education is designed deliberately to increase black self-esteem. black and white critics of African-centered education argue that such a goal is unrealistic and degrades history.

But Molefi Kete-Asante, chairman of Temple University's African American studies department and author of *Afrocentricity*, denies that raising self-esteem is the goal of the curriculum. "Nothing I have written has said the aim is to raise self-esteem," he recently told WUSA-TV (Channel 9). "If you provide accurate information, a byproduct would be increased self-esteem."

While several school systems in the Washington area are studying possible implementation of a multicultural curriculum, the District has this year set up a pilot program at Webb Elementary School on Mount Olivet Road NE.

At Webb, Abena Walker, a poet, performer and former D.C. public school teacher, is introducing 10 teachers to a methodology that emerges from Africa. Walker says her method will enrich education for all children, regardless of race.

The class Walker is teaching after school covers curriculum development, policy statement and methodology and is accredited by the D.C. public schools and by Trinity College for graduate credits.

Walker had presented workshops across the country, including at a recent national conference in Atlanta on the "Infusion of African and African American Content in the School Curriculum." Where such scholars as the late Cheikh Anta Diop, Asante, Asa G. Hilliard III, Martin Bernal and John Henrik Clarke have focused on content, getting out accurate historical information, Walker has concentrated on concepts and methodology.

"An African-centered teacher," says Walker, "is one who has internalized the value system that is based on cooperative learning, seeing discipline as lovingly helping children develop self-control, who can think and plan holistically, combining subjects through projects and integrating the arts into those projects."

Walker contends that African-centered education is being adopted and used throughout the country but that the word "African" is not used. "The code words and phrases for the movement include 'cooperative education, teaching and learning,' 'wholistic education,' 'interdisciplinary education,' and 'values education' or 'character-building.'"

She compares that process to the same one that has made jazz "America's music," and not "African American" music anymore. "Africa should be given credit because it has laid the foundation from which these concepts have been extracted," she said.

Having taught and counseled black and white students, Walker says all children are at risk. "White children tell me how troubled they are in the present system of reward and punishment and fragmented classes. All can benefit from the African-centered methodology, which stresses such benefits as logical consequences versus punishment."

The content of Afrocentricity and Walker's methodology ring true. Those advocating Afrocentricity do not claim that Africa was the source of everything good while Europe was the source of everything bad. But they do say that there is a hidden history that must be uncovered and a value system from which everyone can benefit.

Gilliam, Dorothy. (11/19/90). Afrocentric education would benefit all. *The Washington Post*. Section B, pp. 3, 4.

AFROCENTRICITY
NO CAUSE FOR ALARM

It takes note of a long-neglected heritage, and it makes educational sense. When a lot of people, especially white people, hear the word "Afrocentricity," they feel threatened, nervous or both. They shouldn't.

To say that a particular school system or a particular university should be more Afrocentric in its orientation is simply to say that a school system or university that is predominantly African-American should infuse its teaching and learning with cultural and intellectual emphases that reflect the identity and heritage of its dominant constituency: African Americans.

But it does not mean that a particular school system or university should ignore or belittle the heritage of other peoples who have their own stories of struggles and triumphs. Nor does it mean that being Afrocentric excuses a school system or university from teaching its students the basic skills and knowledge they need to succeed in an increasingly complex world. There is, after all, no such thing as "black physics" or "black mathematics" or "black computer science."

In higher education, to take the area I know best, there have always been institutions that reflect and relate to particular constituencies. Brandeis and Yeshiva place a strong emphasis on the culture and experience of the Jewish people. Notre Dame and Georgetown acknowledge their Catholic roots. Vassar and Barnard have long been devoted to the empowerment of women. West Point and the Naval Academy obviously have strong ties to the nation's military establishment. Each of these institutions have its unique flavor, reflecting its unique constituency, and this flavor infuses its teaching and learning. Students of these institutions receive a solid grounding in whatever academic disciplines they choose to study alongside that special something.

No one accuses these institutions of advocating or practicing cultural separatism or of being propaganda mills.

But when advocates of Afrocentricity speak of infusing a curriculum with an orientation that reflects the heritage of people of African descent, all too often that is just what happens. Those making this accusation themselves could face an accusation: of ignorance, ignorance of the rich tradition of special interest institutions in this nation. Indeed, there is nothing "radical" about culturally specific education at all. It is as American as Mom and apple pie.

I speak as one who attended and am now president of an institution that was "Afrocentric" long before the word came into vogue.

As a Howard University student in the '60s, I never took a course in "Afro-American History" or "Afro-American Literature" or anything with a similar title. But in each discipline within which I studied, my teachers made sure we students knew about the contributions African Americans made to the discipline and the impact of the discipline on the lives of African Americans. This fit comfortably alongside our teachers' primary mission — to make sure we mastered the tools of the discipline, thus providing us with a solid foundation for further education and advancement.

Although we students didn't verbalize it this way, my teachers at Howard were "Afrocentric," and they were passing on that "Afrocentric" legacy to us. And yes, their efforts did build up the self-esteem of the young black men and women who sat in those classrooms. But their efforts enriched the lives of Howard students of other racial and ethnic backgrounds who sat in those classrooms as well.

To regard Afrocentricity simply as a means to help African-American youth feel "good about themselves" is to take the narrow view. The key measure of Afrocentricity's validity is that it makes educational sense.

Whether in elementary school or a university campus, students in this nation need to know about the heritage and contributions of people of African descent and of Asian descent and of Latin American descent as well as people of European descent. An education that views the European heritage as central, and, by assumption, as superior, and that views non-European heritages and peripheral, and, by assumption, inferior, is a deficient education. For it fails to prepare our youth for the reality of a world that is increasingly interdependent and a nation that will increasingly be composed of non-white peoples or, the preferred term these days, "people of color."

Afrocentricity isn't about exclusion. It isn't about kente cloth adornments and leather map-of-Africa medallions, although these certainly add verve to one's wardrobe. Afrocentricity is about inclusion, and that is something all people can understand. It's also why, I believe, we'll be hearing about Afrocentricity for some time to come.

Jenifer, Franklyn G. (11/19/90). Afrocentricity is no cause for alarm. *The Washington Post*. Editorial, p. A15.

Teaching Standard English

Taylor (1987, p. 21) recommends that Standard English must be taught from a cultural perspective. Those who learn Standard English must not be forced to abandon their home dialect or language, nor should they be made to regard their dialect as substandard or inferior. Taylor (1986, pp 166-171) recommends an eight-step developmental approach for teaching oral communication. This is a model that can be used to develop communicative competence in Standard English while still preserving the home or community dialect.

Step 1 Maintain a positive attitude toward one's own language. This is the foundation for all that is to come. All varieties of a language are tools for communicating ideas from person to person, so classrooms must reflect a positive atmosphere of respectful listening and enjoyment of the varieties that are heard.

Step 2 Teachers expand awareness of varieties of language by a variety of forms of language. Books, stories, and poems are read in Formal English as well as in various dialects. Accounts can be taped and retold in Standard English or in other dialects. Students discuss regional and social dialects as they are heard on television shows.

Step 3 Students (older students) are encouraged to recognize, label and contrast distinctive features of various dialects. New linguistic and communicative behaviors can be recognized during this step.

Step 4 Students are given instruction that focuses on the underlying meanings (and intentions) associated with particular dialect forms. Nonverbal cues such as "the evil eye" carries a particular meaning whether it is used by a parent or a teacher. The same utterance in two regions of the country may be interpreted as having different meanings. "I need a tonic" in California is usually interpreted to mean that the speaker needs some sort of medicinal stimulant. In New England, the speaker would be asking for a soft drink. Students learn to assess how well their ideas are understood.

Step 5 Students are taught to recognize the situational rules of communication. They learn what is appropriate in any situation by anticipating the reaction of the audience. The situation may range from formal to informal, or interpersonal to mass communication as in recorded video taping or audio taping. The audience may include classmates, teachers, peers, employers, family, and/or community.

Step 6 Students are taught the production of certain language forms in structured situations. The child usually has some type of script that serves as a model to follow. They do choral readings, read poems, and/or plays. As students learn this new language form, they are rewarded for "successive approximations". Whenever a new language form is presented, models must be provided and practice must be included. (See the poem "I Know an Old Lady in Chapter Seven.)

Step 7 Students are taught the production of certain language forms in controlled situations. At this stage the student no longer has a script. Instead, he/she is role-playing, retelling a story, doing repeated readings of a story or poem. Communicative performance is under the speaker's control. The situation is controlled and predetermined. Hopefully the speaker has internalized the language pattern which was practiced in Step 6 to a level which permits spontaneous generation of the patterns when the content of the communication is known in advance. By making the content and the context of the situation predictable, the teacher frees the student to concentrate more effectively on the skills to be practiced.

Step 8 The ultimate goal of the program is for students to determine the linguistic and communicative requirements of the situation, audience or topic for themselves and then proceed to use the form of language that is most appropriate. The students should be able at this stage to generate the required forms in a real-life experience.

The teacher must begin with a basic belief that it is possible to acquire a second dialect. A variety of learning styles and preferences of the learners must be provided. Students must also see the need to learn another dialect. Instruction must be maintained on an oral basis and be made relevant for students by integrating it with the students' experiences.

Bidialectalism and Codeswitching

Bilingualism/Bidialectalism are defined as the ability to communicate by using two different languages or dialects. Essentially, students must be taught that they can achieve competence in both dialects: Standard English and Black Communications. They use Standard English to communicate effectively in an educational setting: in the job market, in the school, to converse with those who speak another language and in social settings that may help them achieve upward mobility. Students develop their communicative competence, knowing how and when to use Black Communications, at home and in their community to promote group cohesion and solidarity and to maintain credibility. Students learn when to switch from one code - the language of the school - to another - the language of the home, or the language of the community - whenever the need arises.

Essentially, Scotton (1978, pp. 71-73) contends that there are four conditions during which speakers switch from one code to another:

1. When there is a lack of knowledge of our dialect or lack of facility in that language on a certain subject so that the speaker switches for certain parts of the conversation; For instance, when a teacher is returning test papers to a class that has scored extremely low on a test and the teacher can think of only one way to describe their performance: "There's only one word I can use to describe your performance on this test - sorry!"

2. When the speaker wants to exclude certain persons from a portion of the conversation if it is known that these persons do not know the language used for switching; Two African American co-workers are talking about their employer and a White co-worker enters and tries to listen in on the conversation. One of the workers might begin to talk in "pig latin" so that the White person does not know what she is saying.

3. For use as a stylistic device to indicate a change in the "tone" of the conversation at a certain point, or to signal the introduction of a subject more or less formal than what had been under discussion; Two teachers are talking in the teacher's lounge about standardized test results as well as how the children in their classes performed. One teacher tells of a boy who did exceptionally well on the test, but this child is difficult to discipline. "Susan scored about average, but Tyrone made the highest score in the class." The other says, "He did? I had him in my class last year." The first teacher says "Yes, that boy git on my *last* nerve, but I am going to recommended him for the class for the gifted."

4. To impress someone with virtuosity in several languages or at least in one prestige language. The female head of the household opens her telephone bill and sees an error of a four hundred dollar telephone call to Japan. She complains openly about the bill to her sister, as she dials the number of the telephone company. But, when she talks to the telephone representative, she uses the most prestigious dialect. "A $400.00 call to Tokyo!!! Ain't nobody I know live in Japan!" Chile, these people crazy if..... Hello, yes, this is Mrs. Lisa Jones, of 4428 Carol Lane. I am calling about my most recent telephone bill..."

Whole Language/Language Experience

Whole language is one of the most recent "buzz words" in education. Although the concept surfaced in the late 80s and early 90s, it is essentially a revitalization of an older concept the language experience approach to teaching. It encompasses the main tenets of Africentricity. This mode of teaching has as its philosophy:

> What children can think about they talk about. What they talk about they can write. What they can write, they can read. What they can read, others can also read (Allen 1976).

The process starts with what children know and utilizes their experiences to teach them by integrating listening, speaking, reading and writing. As in the newer concept, this approach emphasizes the functional aspect of language. Rather than teaching a series of unrelated skills on ditto sheets and in workbooks, whole language begins with a familiar situation or experience and encourages students to talk about the experience. The teacher writes exactly what the students say as they recall or restructure the experience, and their words then become the textbook. Students read their own words and learn phonics, vocabulary and comprehension skills from that text.

Scaffolding

One valuable tenet of the whole language approach is the concept of *scaffolding*. During the process of teaching, the teacher builds a scaffold or safety net around the students. This safety net provides the constant assurance that the teacher will be advocating for the students and that students will not be penalized for their mistakes. The teacher encourages them to take risks, and helps them learn from their mistakes. The teacher models new ways of speaking. The teacher provides the inward motivation that facilitates a students' seeing value in learning Standard English.

Scaffolding reminds me of the process I used when I taught my daughter how to ride a bike. It began with Ronlyn deciding in the fall that she *wanted* a bicycle for Christmas. We looked at bicycles in the catalogues and decided the one most suited for her needs: to ride to her friend's house, to the mall, and to the local store. After she received the bicycle, I went out with her to teach her how to ride it. When she first mounted the bicycle, I stood with her to help her achieve balance. As she moved forward, I moved with her, assuring her that if she started to fall, I would be there to catch her. As she became more adept of balancing and riding, I gradually moved away and just observed her, encouraging her to ride for longer and longer periods by herself until, at last, she no longer needed me to walk with her. She learned to venture out on her own, riding on the sidewalk, riding in the street, riding to school, and riding to the mall. All the time we continued to talk about bicycle safety including riding in traffic and using hand signals.

Teachers must provide this same support system for students as they teach them to use language to communicate with others in speaking as well as in writing. According to Delpit (1988), teachers must teach students how to use the language (culture) of power so that they will be able to fully participate in the mainstream of American life.

Teachers must basically believe that students can learn the language. They must maintain a safety net around the students that will encourage them to experiment with the language. They must teach students how to use the language in a variety of settings, for a variety of reasons with people on many social levels. They must teach students how to talk with their peers, as well as adults. And, when students make mistakes using the language, teachers must not penalize them, but encourage students to learn from their mistakes, always providing positive feedback and engendering independence on the part of the student. As students begin to show signs of independence in using the language, teachers step back and provide them with additional opportunities to demonstrate their independence.

Cooperative Learning

Cooperative learning is a teaching strategy that can take advantage of call-response and the development of communication competence. (See Pine and Hilliard, 1990 and Slavin, 1987.) This small group process integrates immediate feedback, problem-solving, orality, and literacy, and has been used successfully with students of all ages. Cooperative learning involves dividing a given class into heterogeneous groups of three or four and assigning each group a certain amount of time to solve a problem or answer a research question. Group participants offer solutions which are recorded and then reported to the class. The teacher integrates the group solutions by writing responses on a chart or the chalkboard and allowing the entire class time to reflect on a multiplicity of solutions and set priorities.

Research has documented numerous advantages to this teaching strategy: improved problem solving skills, increased motivation, improvement in achievement and attendance, in involvement and the building of oral and written communicative competence. These skills are developed through intense interaction required within the groups. Each group member has a specified role: to lead discussion, to record notes, or to keep participants focused on the task. All must listen and react to one another's suggestions. For every group activity, the individual's roles change so that all members must participate and take their turn assuming each role.

Students have an opportunity to interact with their peers, to express their ideas, transcribe them into print, compare them to those offered by their peers and select appropriate courses of action. With cooperative learning, orality can feed into literacy in creative and constructive ways. (See Heath's, 1983, description of a literacy event, p. 386; Slavin, 1987, and Johnson and Johnson, 1988 for additional suggestions on cooperative learning and de Bono's CoRT Thinking Program that teaches problem-solving strategies through cooperative learning.)

Conclusion

In summary, it is the task of the school, led by the principal, to develop communicative competence in students. Communicative competence involves learning the *rules* of the language such as subject-verb agreement, pluralization, and learning *how to use* the language to perform routine discourse tasks, such as how to begin and end a conversation. Competence must be learned in the accepted language of the dominant culture of the United States, Standard English, for it is the language of education, politics, economics, and upward social mobility. Students must also develop competence in the language of the African American community. To be able to communicate effectively in BC allows the speaker to achieve credibility, to promote group solidarity and ensure cultural acceptance.

An added advantage of dialectal competence is achieved in speaking with ease and clarity. Abena Walker, mentioned earlier in this chapter, recites a poem about Harriet Tubman. There's a line in that poem that reads "Harriet Tubman didn't take no stuff." The sense of the poem would clearly be lost if Walker had said "Harriet Tubman did not take any nonsense" There is comfort in being able to express oneself naturally.

CHAPTER SEVEN
ACTIVITIES AND PROJECTS

Somebody said it couldn't be done but he, with a chuckle, replied that maybe it couldn't, but he would be one that wouldn't say "no" till he tried. So, he buckled right in, with a trace of a grin on his face. If he feared it, he hid it; and started to sing as he tackled the thing that couldn't be done, and he did it!!!

Anonymous

This poem can serve as a motivation for BC speakers, many of whom are easily discouraged when they do not succeed in school. What these discouraged learners could benefit from is an emphasis on *persistence*: staying with a goal or a task until it is accomplished. Those who persist achieve in spite of insurmountable obstacles. Achieving against the odds is a part of the "Black experience". Persistence can be taught. (See *Learning to Persist, Persisting to Learn*, by B.C. Howard, 1987, Washington, DC: Mid-Atlantic Equity Center School of Education.) A very important part of teaching is modeling and consistently encouraging students that they *can* learn, that they can exert some measure of control over their educational progress. The activities and projects in this chapter are designed to be used with teachers and students alike. They have been developed to be completed with the chapters in this text, and carry the following approximate grade/age level designations where applicable: Teacher educators (TE), Adult education (AE), High school (HS), Middle school (MS), Upper elementary (UE), Lower elementary (LE).

I have included an index for convenience in locating activities.

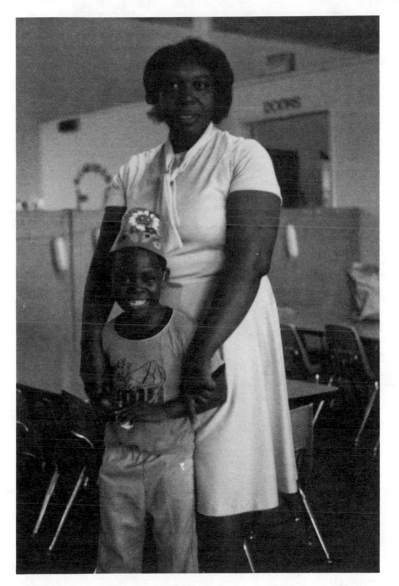

Index to Activities

LE = Lower elementary (K-3)
UE = Upper elementary (4-6)
MS = Middle school (6-8)
HS = High school (9-12)
AE = Adult education
TE = Teacher education

LANGUAGE AND DIALECT (Introduction)

1. **Recognizing Speech Registers** (UE, LE)

Have children roleplay telephone conversations that would use various speech registers. In roleplay, you set the scene.

a) You are talking to your friend who has invited you to a birthday party;

b) You are explaining to the principal why you arrived late for school.

2. **Thinking about culture** (HS, AE, TE)

The process of learning about a dialect begins with learning about your own dialect. Everyone who speaks English speaks a dialect of English. Taylor's *Cross Cultural Communication - An Essential Dimension of Effective Education* suggests that dialect is a product of culture. Why not start thinking about your own culture and then proceed to that of your students? Here are some questions you might ask yourself. Answer these questions first in terms of your own culture and then in terms of the culture of your students.

Family Structure

Who is considered to belong in the family?

What are the rights, roles, and responsibilities of the member?

Interpersonal Relationships

How do people greet each other?

Who may disagree with whom?

How are insults expressed?

Communication

What language and dialects are spoken?

What are the characteristics of speaking "well"?

What roles, attitudes and personality traits are associated with particular aspects of verbal and nonverbal behavior? (pgs. 4,5)

For more details see Taylor's book.

3. **Family Language History** (HS, AE, TE)

Nichols (1989) in her training module, suggests having teachers search their own families' language histories by listing the names of parents, grandparents and other relatives who spoke a language/dialect that was different from others. They may even recall times in their own lives when they had significant experiences with languages/dialects. Have them think about their friends in and out of school, their friends as teenagers, and even their work experiences. Have them compile a list of the people they interacted with. As they think about these people, have them recall the processes they used to acquire their language/dialect. Ask them to write about what they recall and then divide them in groups and have them discuss what they recalled. Are there similarities? differences? Emphasize the idea that language learning can be difficult.

4. **Identifying Regional Expressions** (MS, HS, AE, TE)

Circle the school term you would use to describe the concepts below. This is a portion of the *Checklist of Regional Expressions* prepared by Shuy, found in Clark, Eschholz, and Rosa *Introductory Readings* (New York: St. Martin's Press, 1985), 500-512. Circle the expression *you* use. Suggest others if they are not listed.

1) To be absent from school: bag school, cool, jack, lay out, lie out, play hookey, play truant, run out of school, skip class, skip school, slip off from school, ditch, flick, flake school, blow school, _____

_____

_____

2) Where swings and play areas are: schoolyard, playground, school-ground, yard, grounds, _____

_____

_____

3) An object made of rubber which holds small things together: rubberband, rubberbinder, elastic binder, gum band, elastic band, _____

_____

_____

4) Drinking fountain: cooler, water cooler, bubbler, fountain, drinking fountain, _____

_____

_____

5) The amount of books you can carry in both arms: armful, armload, load, ton, _____

_____

_____

6) Someone from the country: backwoodsman, clodhopper, country gentleman, country jake, hick, yokel, __

_____

_____

7) Become ill: be taken sick, get sick, take sick, taken ill, come down, _____

_____

_____

8) Policeman: cop, copper, fuzz, dick, officer, bull, _____

_____

_____

As an adult/student, share some of the names you would use for these terms with other teachers/students in your school. Are there regional similarities among teachers/students in your school? What do the similarities and differences tell you?

5. **Dialects on TV** (UE, MS, HS, AE, TE)

Conduct a television survey by listening for different dialects on several programs. Keep a chart of what you find. Note the vast differences in dialects even within a given family.

TV PROGRAM	CHARACTER	WORDS/PHRASES	HOW DO YOU SAY IT?
"Different World"			
"227"			
"The Beverly Hillbillies"			
"The Cosby Show"			
"Momma's Place"			
"Fresh Prince of Bel Air"			
"True Colors"			
"Designing Women"			
"Amen"			

131

6. **Pronunciation Study** (TE, AE, HS, MS)

Conduct a pronunciation study. Ask friends and neighbors how they pronounce these words. In order to get a more natural pronunciation, ask the persons you interview to repeat the sentence and fill in the blank.

Question	Pronunciation/Construction	Where this Person Grew Up	Your Pronunciation
What do you call a small stream of water that runs through a farm? (creek)			
Melted animal fat is very _____. (greasy)			
The name of Jesus' mother is _____. (Mary)			
When you want a person to have a good Christmas you say _____ Christmas. (Merry)			
To become united in matrimony is to _____. (marry)			
The top cover of a building is the _____. (roof)			

133

7. Speech styles or registers (TE, AE, HS, MS, UE)

Complete the chart below with the appropriate speech register. Have students volunteer additional examples.

Formal	Informal	Slang	Dialect
I shall look forward to hearing from you.	— — —	— — —	— — —
— — —	— — —	Look, I mean, really. That is really, really rad!	— — —
— — —	— — —	— — —	It bees that way sometime.
— — —	I can't wait to get back to school.	— — —	— — —

TEACHERS' LINGUISTIC ATTITUDES (Chapter I)

1. **Exploring oral expression** (LE, UE, MS, HS, AE, TE)

Encourage your students to explore the full range of vocal expression by having them portray various characters in roleplaying situations. Elementary school students could play the part of Charlotte or Wilbur or Templeton, all of whom probably had very different voices in E.B. White's *Charlotte's Web*. Middle school students could play the role of Bigger, his sister Vera, or Mamma or Buddy in *Native Son*, by Richard Wright. The chapter that describes the rat contains much good dialogue with many opportunities for different characters. High school students could select dialogue from any of Virginia Hamilton's novels: *MC Higgins, The Great, The House of Dies Drear* or any of the series *Justice and Her Brothers, Dustland,* or *The Gathering*. Help students to explore variations in pitch (highness or lowness), in sound, and stress or emphasis in speaking.

2. **Listening to dialects** (AE, TE)

Select the one child in your classroom who speaks a dialect that is most different from your dialect. Tape record a five-10-minute segment as he/she uses the dialect then transcribe the tape. Note differences and similarities not just in the sounds, but more importantly in word order (syntax), word meaning, and word choice (semantics). How do they differ from yours? How are they similar to your dialect?

3. **Improving speaking skills** (UE, MS, HS, AE, TE)

Select diagrams, models, and pictures from content area texts (social studies, math, science), and have students explain the illustrations to one another in cooperative groups. (See Chapter Six.) They can develop step-by-step lists and written descriptions of key concepts. They could use these lists and descriptions as study guides when preparing for tests.

4. **Books about African Americans** (LE, UE, MS, HS, AE, TE)

The following books include dialect renderings, and they portray African American children in a positive light. It is most important that teachers take a portion of *every day* to read aloud to children. Ten to 15 minutes is sufficient. Start a book and continue it for an entire week. Ask questions about the characters in the book. Have children write different endings and write dialogues between characters. Your students can respond to the book in many different ways. Books can be adapted to teach and reinforce all subject areas. Before you read each book, chart its uses. Possibilities are limitless. (For additional titles see Appendix A.)

Book Chart

Book Title and Author	Reading	English	Math	Science	Social Studies
Flossie and the Fox by Patricia McKissack	Teach sequential order–who Flossie met as she journeyed to the McKutchen Farm	Have children write the formal, informal and slang rendition of Flossie's speech	Talk about proving addition and subtraction problems	Construct semantic feature comparing the features of foxes, cats, squirrels, their appearances, habitats, food sources	Describe Flossie's qualities: She has set a goal and lets nothing stop her from reaching it

Art: Illustrations are vivid in this book. Have students describe Flossie's nonverbal expressions.

Clifton, L. *My Brother Fine With Me*. New York: Holt, Rinehart and Winston, 1975. (LE)

This is the story of a little boy, Baggy, who decides to run away and receives help from his sister. This story is written in dialect.

Greenfield, E. *Honey I Love and Other Poems*. New York: Thomas Y. Crowell, 1978. (LE, UE)

This book is filled with warm, positive poems that African American children can identify with. It is illustrated by Leo and Diane Dillon. (Check other titles by Greenfield for additional excellent examples.)

Mathis, S.B. *The Hundred Penny Box*. New York: Scholastic Incorporated (1989 printing), 1975.

This is a heart-warming story about a boy and his grandmother, who has saved a penny for every year of her life. Each penny holds an interesting account of the events that took place in her life.

McKissack, P. *Flossie and the Fox*. New York: Dial Books for Young Readers, 1986. ISBN: 0-8037-02050-7 (LE, UE)

A wily fox notorious for stealing eggs meets his match when he encounters a bold little girl in the woods who insists upon proof that he is a fox before she will be frightened. This book is good for teaching sequence and dialogue. (Check other titles by McKissack for additional excellent examples.)

Myers, W.D. *Won't Know Til' I Get There*. New York: Puffin Books, 1988. (UE, MS, HS)

Fourteen-year-old Stephen, his new foster brother, and his friends are sentenced to help out an old-age home for the summer, after Stephen is caught writing graffiti on a train. Stephen keeps a journal of his humorous escapades. Myers is known for his humor and rich use of language. Most of Myers' books are written for upper elementary, middle and high school students. (Check other titles by Myers for excellent examples.)

5. **An Alternative to Round Robin Reading** (AE, TE)

Round robin reading (RRR) or barbershop reading is the negative practice of having every student sit with a book opened to the same page while one student after another reads aloud in a predicted sequence. This common practice reinforces word-by-word reading by placing undue emphasis upon calling words (as Alice was doing.) RRR deemphasizes reading for meaning, because it focuses attention on the *pronunciation* of words rather than the *communication* of the author's meaning. Woods (1983) offers alternatives: The entire class, all boys, all girls, a specific row pairs or other small groups can read aloud in unison. The teachers should select sentences or groups of sentences for special emphasis: (1) imitative reading during which the teacher reads first and students imitate to demonstrate intonation patterns in dialogue; (2) the entire class reading the definition of important concepts; (3) assisted reading, during which a less proficient reader reads with slightly more proficient readers; and (4) mumble reading during which all students read aloud (to themselves) at their own pace for a better understanding of a concept or idea. Those alternatives give more students the opportunity to read aloud, does not single one child out for embarrassment and emphasizes reading as a communication tool for a particular purpose. Remember: *No student should read aloud what he/she has not first read silently!*

6. **Miscue Analysis** (TE) First developed by Kenneth and Yetta Goodman, miscue analysis involves a careful look at the expected response (what is written) and the observed response (what is read). The errors are written in the text.

Maxie lived in three small rooms on the top-~~floor~~ *flour* of an

old brownstone ~~house~~ *horse* on Orange ~~Street~~ *Skreet* She had ~~lived~~ *live*

there for many ~~years~~ *year*, and everyday ~~was~~ the same for

Maxie. Every morning at exactly at 7:10, ~~Maxie's little~~ *Maxie large*

orange cat ~~jumped~~ *jump* onto the windowsill and ~~skretched~~ *skretch* out

in the morning sun.

Expected Response	Observed Response	Effect on Text
floor	flour	change of meaning
house	horse	change of meaning
street	skreet	no meaning change (dialect shift - a alternation of skr for str)
had lived	live	no meaning change (dialect shift - verbs stay the same)
years	year	no meaning change (dialect shift - nouns remain the same)
was	was is omitted	no meaning change (dialect shift - form of be is omitted to show condition)
large	little	change of meaning
stretched	skretch	no meaning change (dialect shift - alternation of skr for str)

Notice, those miscues that do not change the meaning of the sentence are consistent with the sounds, structure and word order of the dialect. See Chapter Four for more on distinctive features.

7. **Black Communications in literature** (UE, MS)

Sharon Bell Mathis' book, *The Hundred Penny Box* (Scholastic 1989), is about a young boy's relationship with his grandmother, Mathis includes many examples of BC:

"The ice cream be melted fore you get home." p. 10 (be as future tense)

"And baby, baby-sweet woman, you doing fine. Everything you doing is right. p.11 (Omission of the verb "to be")

"What you mamma name?" p. 20 (Omission of the 's and r at the end of the word)

"But he just looking at me, just looking and standing." p.24 (Omission of the verb "to be")

"How you going to hide a house?" p.24 (Omission of verb "to be")

"This child and me just talking." p. 28 (Omission of verb "to be")

Teachers could have students read the dialogue as it is and then rewrite the dialogue in Standard English. They could discuss the value of both dialects.

BC and AFRICAN ORIGINS (Chapters II and III)

1. Capitalizing on Call-Response (LE, UE, MS, HS, AE, TE)

Since call-response is such an integral part of the oral tradition, teachers can use the process to encourage oral responses. Call-response is an effective instructional tool because it requires immediate feedback from children. Smitherman (1977) categorizes responses according to their purpose. As you talk with your students, teach them how to respond as a group in a variety of ways. For instance, you may use a poem such as "A Dream Deferred" by Langston Hughes, and have them repeat each line after you (repetition). Or, you might make response cards with *yes* printed on one side and *no* printed on the other. As you ask them questions, have them respond by showing the appropriate side of the card (cosigning). Here are Smitherman's categories, along with definitions, examples in Black Communications and sample applications for classroom use (p. 107).

Categories of Responses:

Cosigning: Agreeing with the speaker "Yes"; "I hear you"; "well" Use response cards or thumbs up sign.

Encouraging: Urging the speaker to continue; "That's right", "keep going" Tap index and middle finger on palm of other hand to show encouragement, or use this tapping to show how many syllables are in a word.

Completer: Completing the speaker's statement as requested or spontaneously.

Speaker: "I'm just gonna wait" - Response: "'till my change come"

Teacher says the first part of a rule or generalization and students say the last part.

Repetition: Using same words speaker has said. Have students memorize poems that have repetitive phrases.

OnT (time): Acknowledging that what the speaker has said is timely and to the point - "Shonuff," "ooooo-weeee!," or giving skin, permit students to openly affirm or agree.

[Smitherman's categories of Call-response, p. 107.]

2. **A quiz on culture.** (TE, AE) Taylor has published "What Do I Know About Culture, Communication and Language." Take this quiz and determine how much you know.

What Do I Know About Culture, Communication, And Language?

Directions: Circle A for each statement with which you agree or D for each statement with which you disagree.

A D 1. One's culture and one's race are usually one and the same.

A D 2. Culture consists primarily of a groups' arts, music, dance, food, language, and dress.

A D 3. Cultural groups are generally mutually exclusive of one another.

A D 4. Cultural traits tend to have a genetic base.

A D 5. In general, people who speak the same language are members of the same cultural group.

A D 6. People are often unaware of some of the rules of their culture.

A D 7. Culture is expressed exclusively by one's verbal behavior.

A D 8. The only significant components of one's communication system are pronunciation rules, vocabulary, and grammatical rules.

A D 9. Standard English is the correct way to speak at all times.

A D 10. There are universal norms for acceptable communicative behavior within the United States.
A D 11. If a student violates the school's cultural or communicative norms, it is usually as an act of defiance.
A D 12. In general, speaking a nonstandard dialect suggests low cognitive development.
A D 13. Standard English has more and better structures than other varieties of English.
A D 14. Most standardized tests are based on rules of English used in all linguistic groups.
A D 15. Standard English is White English.
A D 16. In general, students from poor families do not communicate as well as those from middle class families.
A D 17. In general, Black students do not communicate as well as White students.
A D 18. Parents who do not speak Standard English should avoid talking to their children to prevent them from developing poor speech habits.
A D 19. If a child is to learn Standard English, he/she must unlearn any other variety of English that he/she speaks.
A D 20. Black American English is by definition a nonstandard variety of English.

Answers: Each statement reflects a common myth of stereotype pertaining to communication or culture. Therefore, you should have disagreed with each one.

O. Taylor, *Cross Cultural Communication - An Essential Dimension of Effective Education* (Washington, DC: Mid-Atlantic Center for Race Equity, 1987) p. 2. Used with permission.

3. **Curriculum based on self-esteem** (LE, UE, MS, HS) Folami Prescott and Jawanza Kunjufu have developed Self-Esteem Through Culture Leads To Academic Excellence (SETCLAE), a African-based curriculum model designed to motivate students. The curriculum includes pre and post-tests, lesson plans, workbooks, adult and children's books, videos, certificates, posters, and con-

sultants for in-service training. It can be ordered from African American Images, Chicago.

4. **Resource book** (LE, UE, MS, HS, AE, TE) *African American Baseline Essays* and lesson plans (revised Spring, 1990), has a wealth of information about the contributions of Africans and African Americans in the areas of art, language arts, math, science, social studies, and music. Teachers can use the easy-to-read text as a reference source. (Portland Public Schools)

5. **Memorizing Poetry** (LE, UE, MS) Janice Hale-Benson's research has pointed out several curricular implications for African American children with emphasis on: speaking, listening, labeling, storytelling, chanting, imitating, and reciting should be encouraged (p. 161). Use a book of poems such as *Honey, I Love and Other Poems* by Eloise Greenfield (1978) as a start and have children read and memorize the poems.

6. **A child's book about Africa** (MS, UE, LE) Atlantis and Anthony Browder have written *My First Trip to Africa*, a true story told by a seven-year-old who travels to Egypt. The book chronicles her experiences during a 13-day study tour and is written for children to help in understanding personal history, world history, and African history. A parent/teacher guide is included. Institute of Karmic Guidance, Washington, DC.

7. **Audiocassette tapes on African contributions** (HS, AE, TE) Jacquelina L. Van Sertima has developed *Legacies* - ten 90 minute audio cassette tapes that compliment a series of books edited by Ivan Van Sertima. These tapes are appropriate for high school and adult populations. They can be ordered from (Legacies, Highland Park, NJ.). Listen to them as you drive to and from work or school. There is much you can learn about African contributions to world history.

8. **Street games.** (LE, UE) Mays (1980) describes African-oriented singing games that employ synchronization of body as well as hand movements and words and are played mainly by girls between the ages of 5 and 7. These

games test preciseness, hand and speech coordination, and the ability to keep in rhythm. They are played outside, mainly where there are large concentrations of poor children, and they use the dialect. Children who have otherwise been labeled "nonverbal" are most adept at chanting the syncopated rhythms and demonstrating linguistic competence. Mays recommends that teachers tape the games and use them as a basis for teaching.

1. Teach rhyming words by writing the words used in the game on cards and illustrating them and developing a matching game.
2. Write in (Standard English) descriptions of hand movements used in the games.
3. Create new street games in Standard English and have children write them.
4. Develop vocabulary skills by incorporating new words into new street games(pp. 76-82).

See *Apples on a Stick, The Folklore of Black Children* (1983).

9. **Books about street games** (LE, UE, MS) Joanna Cole and Stephanie Calmenson have written *Miss Mary Mack and Other Children's Street Games* (New York: Morrow Junior Books, 1990). It contains a collection of rhymes used in street games. They include hand-clapping, ball-bouncing, counting out, and just-for-fun rhymes along with teases and comebacks. Two students could read this book together and share examples with the class.

10. **Learning about the history of slavery** (MS, HS, AE) For a graphic description of "the middle passage" and a slave who seized an entire ship and tried to return to Africa see "Joseph Cinque and the Amistad Mutiny" *New Golden Legacy Illustrated History Magazine*, 1983. Volume 10.

11. **An alphabet book for Black children** (LE Preschool) Mia Issac has written *AlphaBlack Culture Beginning Activity Book*. It's a personal vision of how to develop self-esteem and Black consciousness in young children. This very colorful book makes suggestions for parents to place a picture of their children on each page from A to Z. (IGIA, Columbia, SC).

12. **Learning about the Gullah** (UE, MS, HS, AE, TE)
For interesting facts about the Gullah people and their language, read *The Gullah: People Blessed by God* by Llaila Olela Afrika, a naturopathist, historian, author, and lecturer. This 38-page book commemorates the Gullah Festival held in Beaufort, South Carolina on the weekend preceding Memorial Day. The book reveals little known facts including the Gullah relationship with Indians, Gullah proverbs, stories, and technology. (Goldenseal, Beaufort, SC)

USING DISTINCTIVE FEATURES (Chapter IV)

1. Working with language (LE, UE)
Children learn about language structure by using it. They need to handle it, manipulate and it, and play with the language to find out what it will and will not do. Listen for the one socially stigmatized structure you find most frequently in use in your region; for example, third person singular. Make a set of linguistic blocks by covering milk cartons with paint or construction paper. On all sides of one block write words that can serve as subjects: she, Tyrone, Shirley, the dog. On another block write verbs that agree: cries, walks, runs, cares, etc. Have students make sentences by manipulating the blocks and writing down the sentences they develop. Then have them change subjects and verbs for agreement. Additional sets of blocks can contain adverbs and adjectives. Sentence patterns (noun, verb, adjective, adverb) could be developed from this manipulation of words. Designate one color of block for each part of speech. Nouns can be green, verbs red, etc. For older children print words on varied colored construction paper and put all nouns in one bag, verbs in another and so on. Students can select one word from each bag and construct a sentence.

2. Listening for stigmatized forms (MS, HS, AE, TE)
Make a list of the sounds and structures that are most often considered socially stigmatized in your region of the country. Compare them to those listed in Chapter Five. Answer the following questions: Why are the forms socially stigmatized? Does anyone else other than African Americans use the form? If you have found others using the form, try to describe the situation and/or setting in which they are used. Describe situations in

which the use of socially stigmatized forms would be appropriate.

3. **Homophonous Pronunciations** (HS, AE, TE)

The following is a list of words that sound alike because of dialect/language. Some are regional and others are social dialects. How many can you add to the list?

whether/rather	boil/ball
told/tole	bar/bear
sold/sole/soul	down/Don
oil/earl	scrip/strip
our/are	strip(t)/script

Teachers should be careful not to use these words on worksheets or tests. They confuse the students. The differences in spelling and pronunciation should be pointed out to students.

4. **Recognizing dialect shift** (TE)

A dialect shift is a translation without a loss in comprehension. The dialect rendition must be one of the distinctive features of the dialect applied to the expected response in Standard English. The table below lists Johnson's (1975) examples. As dialect speakers read, they translate the expected response into their dialectal repertoire. The observed response must be consistent with BC sound and/or structure.

Dialect Shifts

Expected Responses	Observed Responses	Explanation
They wanted the ball.	They want the ball.	Verbs usualy retain the same form in tense.
He does his work.	He do his work.	Verbs usually retain the same form in person.
She has five dolls.	She have five doll.	Plurality is expressed once in a sentence.
He usually is working.	He be working.	Be is used to show a condition that is an everyday occurrence.
He is sick	He sick.	Be is omitted to show a temporary condition.
He is late for school today.	He late for school.	Be is omitted to show a temporary condition.
The man's hat was lost.	The man hat was lost.	Possession is shown by proximity.

K. Johnson, "Black Dialect Shift in Oral Reading," *Journal of Reading* (April, 1975) pp. 535-540.

5. **Usage Lesson** (AE, HS, MS, UE) Ross and Roe (1990) provide a good activity for emphasizing the need for correct usage where dialect is concerned. Write out a dialogue between an employer and a person who is interviewing for a position. Divide the class into cooperative groups of three. Give them three to five minutes to read the dialogue and decide whether the interviewee should get the position. Make the dialogue realistic, using slang, BC and street talk. Then have each group rewrite the interview in Standard English.

CAPITALIZING ON VERBAL STRATEGIES (Chapter V)

1. **Questions for teacher educators** (TE) After reading Chapter V, pose these questions to teacher educators. Place them in cooperative groups and let them develop answers to the questions. At the end of the session they can share answers.

   a. What reasons might you use to appeal to adolescents who use the verbal strategies to become bidialectal?
   b. Should teachers approach the teaching of language arts to culturally different learners any differently than they do to other children? Why or why not?
   c. Should teachers use these same verbal strategies as the students do? Why or why not?

2. **Call-response in everyday music** (MS, HS, AE, TE) Have students bring in records and tapes that illustrate call/response as it is used in music. Be sure to include gospel music, jazz, rock, reggae, and rap music.

3. **Call-response on tape** (HS, AE, TE) View the video-tape "American Tongues" and answer the following questions.

   a. How many different dialects exist in the United States?
   b. Do any of the African Americans on the tape use call-response? Cite examples of call-response.
   c. Are there any examples of verbal strategies that are used by other cultures on this tape?
   d. Are there any examples of the dilemma between talking a special way and being ridiculed by peers? Cite specific instances.

4. Solving problems with verbal strategies (HS, MS) Foster provides good examples of how a teacher's lack of information about the language of the students can cause problems. Talk about what you might do if you were faced with Foster's "Reality 25."

> This incident took place in an inner-city language arts class about a week before the Christmas vacation. During a lull, two Black male students approached their White female teacher and asked, "Miss Frank, what does 'trim' mean?"

> Miss Frank, unsuspectingly, responded with "Oh, I guess to hang ornaments on the Christmas tree." With that, one youngster turned to his friend, grinned, put out his hand for some skin, and the class burst into laughter.

5. Studying students' language. (MS, HS, TE) Secure Foster's Jive Lexicon Analogy Test, Series 1, and administer it to a group of in-service teachers of middle and high school students. This could be the introduction for a series of discussions for faculty study on the language of the students. Teachers need to become familiar with the language of students. The test can be secured from H. L. Foster, 100 Sedgemoor Ct., Williamsville, NY 14221.

6. Improvisation (LE, UE, MS, HS, AE, TE) Ross and Roe (1990, p. 172) define improvisation as a dramatic situation without a script. Improvisations are unstructured because they have no clear beginning or end and they can use individuals or small groups. Children and teacher first set up the situation by describing the setting and the topic/concept to be discussed. Improvisation is a good tool for developing movements, feelings, reactions of characters. Many highly aggressive children enjoy improvisation - it is a part of BC. Use improvisation in your classroom and then have children discuss what they have composed. Rap is highly improvised. Students can compose raps or songs that illustrate a concept you have discussed on a character they have read about.

7. Survey for teacher education (TE) It is important that teachers begin to watch and listen to how people use language. Conduct a survey of television programs that have adolescent African American males. Make a note of the verbal strategies they use.

Survey of Television Programs

TV Program	Character	Strategy	Example
"Amen"			
"Fresh Prince of Bel Air"			
"Blossom"			
"A Different World"			
"The Cosby Show"			

8. **Interviewing strategy users** (MS, HS) Interview a group of African American males and have them give you the local names for the three strategies described in the article. Have them demonstrate each one.

Interview a group of African American males who use the strategies. Find out how they feel about using Standard English. Ask them these questions: What is Standard English? When would you use it? How might you use Standard English to help you? Give the names of people you know who use both Standard English and Black Communications.

9. **Using rap in positive ways** (MS, HS) Direct a group of students in producing and performing in a rap video that summarizes a book or describes a concept they have learned. Use cooperative learning groups that work on writing the script, selecting the scenery and the music and directing the performance. Have the best rappers take a leadership role in each group. Videotape the presentations.

10. **Testing verbal strategies** (MS, HS) E.A. Smith (1974) has written a test of verbal strategies and it is included in his dissertation. Even though the test is nearly 20 years old, some of the strategies are still in common use in various parts of the country.

11. **Rap in literature** (MS, HS, AE) Author Walter Dean Myers is known for his humor and the use of BC in his books. *The Mouse Rap* is a story of a fourteen-year-old Frederick Douglas and his streetwise friends who love to play basketball. They search for a hidden treasure from the days of Al Capone. The setting of the book is Harlem, portrayed (at last) as an ordinary city neighborhood. Myers uses rap throughout the novel - at the beginning of each chapter and to begin and end the book.

(Perma-Bound, Jacksonville, IL).

Chm chm chmm, De De Dee
What's gotta be, gotta be-be-be
Don't run no jive, don't sing no blues
I just TCB and pay my dues

'Cause I'm the table topper, the stardust dropper
The neat Tip-Topper and the Fleet Hip-Hopper
You've heard my story, you've dug my show
You've rapped the rhythm and felt the flow
But now it's time for the Mouse to split
'Cause the tale is ended when the pieces fit
Chm chm chmmm, De De Dee
What's gotta be, gotta be-be-be
Yes!

BUILDING COMMUNICATIVE COMPETENCE (Chapter VI)

Activities for language function
1. **Roleplaying** (LE, UE, MS, HS)

Help students determine that language varies according to the audience and the purposes for any given situation of the speaker. Set up this roleplaying situation involving a male. Two males were fighting on the playground. They were surrounded by a large, noisy crowd that was cheering them on. Choose a variety of audiences to roleplay with the male as he describes the incident to a variety of audiences: (1) a little girl three years younger than he; (2) a group of his peers; (3) the classroom's teacher; and (4) the principal. Each situation should require a different form of communication. Before the players act out each situation, have them decide on the register of language that will be most appropriate for each audience as well as give examples of words, phrases, and gestures that could be used most effectively with each audience.

Incident	Audience	Speech Register	Words, Phrases & Gestures
Two males fighting on the school playground.	Peers		
	Little girl		
An onlooker describes what he saw.	Teacher		
	Principal		

2. Practice using -ed on Past Tense forms (LE, UE, AE)

Here is a poem that can be used by teachers to help students hear as well as say -ed on past tense forms. Depending on their grade levels, students can listen to the poem being read, read it themselves, or memorize it while focusing on the past tense. The repetition of -ed helps to reinforce the tense as well as the sound.

I Know an Old Lady

I know an old lady who swallowed a fly,
I don't know why she swallowed a fly,
I guess she'll die!

I know an old lady who swallowed a spider,
That wriggled and wriggled and tickled inside her.
She swallowed the spider to catch the fly.
But I don't know why she swallowed the fly!
I guess she'll die.

I know an old lady who swallowed a bird,
Now how absurd, to swallow a bird!
She swallowed a bird to catch the spider
That wriggled and wriggled and tickled inside her.
She swallowed the spider to catch the fly,
But I don't know why she swallowed the fly!
I guess she'll die!

I know an old lady who swallowed a cat.
Now fancy that, to swallow a cat!
She swallowed the bird to catch the spider
That wriggled and wriggled and tickled inside her.
She swallowed the spider to catch the fly,
But I don't know why she swallowed the fly!
I guess she'll die!

I know an old lady who swallowed a dog.
My, what a hog to swallow a dog!
She swallowed the dog to catch the cat.
She swallowed the cat to catch the bird.
She swallowed the bird to catch the spider
That wriggled and wriggled and tickled inside her.
She swallowed the spider to catch the fly,
But I don't know why she swallowed the fly!

I guess she'll die!

I know an old lady who swallowed a goat
Just opened her throat, and in walked the goat?
She swallowed the goat to catch the dog.
She swallowed the dog to catch the cat.
She swallowed the cat to catch the bird.
She swallowed the bird to catch the spider
That wriggled and wriggled and tickled inside her.
She swallowed the spider to catch the fly,
But I don't know why she swallowed the fly!
I guess she'll die!

I know an old lady who swallowed a cow.
I don't know how she swallowed a cow.
She swallowed the cow to catch the goat.
She swallowed the goat to catch the dog.
She swallowed the dog to catch the cat.
She swallowed the cat to catch the bird.
She swallowed the bird to catch the spider.
That wriggled and wriggled and tickled inside her.
She swallowed the spider to catch the fly,
But I don't know why she swallowed the fly!
I guess she'll die!

I know an old lady who swallowed a HORSE!
She's dead, OF COURSE!

Anonymous

3. **Codeswitching practice** (LE, UE, MS, HS, AE, TE)
Set up a series of roleplaying exercises that require speakers to switch between one dialect and another. Use Scotton's four reasons and have the participants meet in cooperative groups and brainstorm to develop situations for which each of the four reasons would apply. See the examples that were presented in Chapter Six for ideas.

1. Lack of knowledge of one dialect
2. To exclude certain persons from a portion of the conversation
3. As a stylistic device to change the tone of the conversation

4. To impress someone with virtuosity in several dialects

4. **Pattern books for specific structures** (UE, LE) Pattern books that offer repetitive sentences may be used to assist younger students with certain SE constructions. They require oral reading and repetition with teachers and students.

a) *Ask Mr. Bear* can be used to develop the possessive pattern.

b) *The Very Hungry Caterpillar* can be used to develop plurals.

c) *I Know an Old Lady that Swallowed a Fly* is especially helpful for the past tense pattern.

5. **From another point of view** (UE, MS, HS, TE) Often it is difficult to see something from the point of view of another person. Teachers and students alike need to be able to appreciate the language that is used by others. Here is an example of how you might begin to sympathize with the other side of a story. First, review the story of the "Three Little Pigs" with your audience by having them retell the story: A big, bad wolf ate the three little pigs by huffing and puffing and blowing each of their houses down. Then read *The True Story of the Three Little Pigs* by A. Wolf as told to John Scieszka (1989). (Viking Penguin, New York) In this story, the wolf gives his own version of what really happened when he met with the three pigs. He also clearly refers to one of the pigs who talks about his grandmother. Beautifully illustrated and extremely hilarious! Note: I met Jon Sciezka and asked him what prompted the reference to talking about someone's grandmother, and he stated that he probably got it from his neighborhood in Brooklyn where talking about female relatives was a sensitive subject to many people who live there.

6. **Cognitive Mapping** (LE, UE, MS, HS, TE) Cognitive mapping is another instructional strategy that capitalizes on the concept of relevance and integration in the African world view. A cognitive map (or web) represents a verbal picture of ideas or concepts which are organized and symbolized by the reader. Maps can take many different forms: topical or linear, sunburst or spider, a

flow chart format or a leaning tree.

Figure 2 in the chapter on Black Communications that illustrates BC as a system is a map.

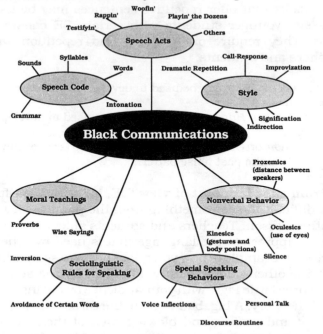

FIGURE 2. Black Communications is not just a speech code. It is a system of communication.

A cognitive map communicates with the reader by just utilizing key concepts and words. It illustrates the relationships between concepts. Any information that can fit into a conventional outline can be placed on a map. Maps can be used in prereading to develop background before reading. They can be used in prewriting to illustrate concepts that will be used in a paragraph. They can be used to illustrate the main idea and in teaching other comprehension skills. Maps are an aid that can be used to develop oral language. For instance, after a student has read a book, he can illustrate the characters, setting, plot, and theme. In the oral report, the student can use the map and explain what has been read.

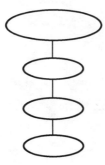

Sequential order

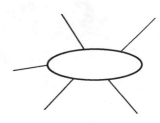

Main idea with details

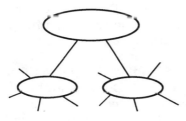

Comparison — Contrast

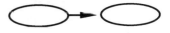

Cause — Effect

The format used in a map is dependent upon the way the author organizes his/her ideas.

APPENDIX A

Children Must See Themselves in Books

I remember as a child reading books like *The Little Engine that Could*, the Pearl Buck Books, *Heidi*, and the entire Nancy Drew mystery series. Those were good books. In those days, there weren't many opportunities for Black children to identify with the main character of the stories because virtually all of the stories were about Whites. It was not until I read *Native Son*, *The Color Purple*, autobiographies of Frederick Douglas and Malcolm X that I could actually see myself as a story character. Children need to read and to have books read to them that help them identify with the hero and the heroines. They need to see themselves as inventors, adventurers, problem-solvers and real live people who have the same hopes and dreams as the characters on paper. Indeed, for these same reasons, children from all cultures also need to read these kinds of books.

The Coretta Scott King Award and Honor Books are just a beginning list of suggested books for children and adults. These awards are presented annually to African American authors and illustrators whose books promote an understanding and appreciation of the culture and contribution of all people to the realization of the American dream. The award commemorates the life and work of Martin Luther King, Jr., and honors his widow, Coretta Scott King, for her courage and determination in continuing the work for peace and world brotherhood. These award-winning authors and illustrators have penned many other books that would also make for outstanding reading.

The following reprint of the awards used with permission lists the authors, book title, and publisher in parentheses.

1990

Patricia & Frederick McKissack, *A Long Hard Journey: The Story of the Pullman Porter* (Walker)

Honor Books

Eloise Greenfield, *Nathaniel Talking* (Black Butterfly)
Virginia Hamilton, *The Bells of Christmas* (Harcourt)
Lillie Patterson, *Martin Luther King, Jr., and the Freedom Movement* (Facts on File)

1989

Walter Dean Myers, *Fallen Angels* (Scholastic)

Honor Books

James Berry, *A Thief in the Village and Other Stories* (Orchard)
Virginia Hamilton, Anthony Burns: *The Defeat and Triumph of a Fugitive Slave (Knopf)*

1988

Mildred D. Taylor,*The Friendship* (Dial)

Honor Books

Alexis De Veaux, *An Enchanted Hair Tale* (Harper)
Julius Lester, *The Tale of Uncle Remus: The Adventures of Brer Rabbit (*Dial)

1987

Mildred Pitts Walter, *Justin and the Best Biscuits in the World* (Lothrop)

Honor Books

Ashley Bryan, *Lion and the Ostrich Chicks and Other African Folk Tales* (Atheneum)
Joyce Hansen, *Which Way Freedom?* (Walker)

1986

Virginia Hamilton, *The People Could Fly: American Black Folktales* (Knopf)

Honor Books

Virginia Hamilton, *Junius Over Far* (Harper)
Mildred Pitts Walter, *Trouble's Child* (Lothrop)

1985

Walter Dean Myers, *Motown and Didi* (Viking)

Honor Books

Candy Dawson Boyd, *Circle of Gold* (Apple/Scholastic)
Virginia Hamilton, *A Little Love* (Philomel)

1984

Lucille Clifton, *Everett Anderson's Goodbye* (Holt)

Special Citation

Coretta Scott King, compiler, *The Words of Martin Luther King, Jr.* (Newmarket Press)

Honor Books

Virginia Hamilton, *The Magical Adventures of Pretty Pearl* (Harper)
James Haskins, *Lena Horne* (Coward-McCann)
Joyce Carol Thomas, *Bright Shadow* (Avon)
Mildred Pitts Walter, *Because We Are* (Lothrop)

1983

Virginia Hamilton, *Sweet Whispers, Brother Rush* (Philomel)

Honor Books

Julius Lester, *This Strange New Feeling* (Dial)

1982

Mildred D. Taylor, *Let the Circle Be Unbroken* (Dial)

Honor Books

Alice Childress, *Rainbow Jordan* (Coward-McCann)
Kristin Hunter, *Lou in the Limelight* (Scribner)
Mary E. Mebane, *Mary: An Autobiography* (Viking)

1981

Sidney Poitier, *This Life* (Knopf)

Honor Books

Alexis De Veaux, *Don't Explain: A Song of Billie Holiday* (Harper)

1980

Walter Dean Myers, *The Young Landlords* (Viking)

Honor Books

Berry Gordy, *Movin' Up* (Harper)
Eloise Greenfield & Lessie Jones Little, *Childtimes: A Three-Generation Memoir* (Harper)
James Haskins, *Andrew Young: Young Man with a Mission* (Lothrop)
James Haskins, *James Van Der Zee: The Picture Takin' Man* (Dodd)
Ellease Southerland, *Let the Lion Eat Straw* (Scribner)

1979

Ossie Davis, *Escape to Freedom: A Play about Young Frederick Douglass* (Viking)

Honor Books

Carol Fenner, *Skates of Uncle Richard* (Random)
Virginia Hamilton, *Justice and Her Brothers* (Greenwillow)
Lillie Patterson, *Benjamin Banneker* (Abingdon Press)

Jeanne W. Peterson, *I Have a Sister, My Sister Is Deaf* (Harper)

1978

Eloise Greenfield, *Africa Dream* (Crowell)

Honor Books

William J. Faulkner, *The Days When the Animals Talked: Black Folk Tales How They Came to Be* (Follett)
Frankcina Glass, *Marvin and Tige* (St. Martin's)
Eloise Greenfield, *Mary McCleod Bethune* (Crowell)
James Haskins, *Barbara Jordan* (Dial)
Lillie Patterson, *Coretta Scott King* (Garrard)
Ruth Ann Stewart, *Portia: The Life of Portia Washington Pittman, The Daughter of Booker T. Washington* (Doubleday)

1977

James Haskins, *The Story of Stevie Wonder* (Lothrop)

Honor Books

Lucille Clifton, *Everett Anderson's Friend* (Holt)
Mildred D. Taylor, *Roll of Thunder, Hear My Cry* (Dial)
Clarence N. Blake & Donald F. Martin, *Quiz Book on Black America* (Houghton)

1976

Pearl Bailey, *Duey's Tale* (Harcourt)

Honor Books

Shirley Graham, *Julius K. Nyerere: Teacher of Africa* (Messner)
Eloise Greenfield, *Paul Robeson* (Crowell)
Walter Dean Myers, *Fast Sam, Cool Clyde and Stuff* (Viking)
Mildred Taylor, *Song of the Trees* (Dial)

1975

Dorothy Robinson, *The Legend of Africania* (Johnson Publishing)

1974

Sharon Bell Mathis, *Ray Charles* (Crowell)

Honor Books

Alice Childress, *A Hero Ain't Nothin' but a Sandwich* (Coward-McCann)
Lucille Clifton, *Don't You Remember?* (Dutton)
Louise Crane, *Ms. Africa: Profiles of Modern African Women* (Lippincott)
Kristin Hunter, *Guest in the Promised Land* (Scribner)
John Nagenda, *Mukasa* (Macmillan)

1973

Alfred Duckett, *I Never Had It Made: The Autobiography of Jackie Robinson* (Putnam)

1972

Elton C. Fax, *17 Black Artists* (Dodd)

1971

Charlemae Rollins, *Black Troubadour: Langston Hughes* (Rand McNally)

Honor Books

Maya Angelou, *I Know Why the Caged Bird Sings* (Random)
Shirley Chisholm, *Unbought and Unbossed* (Houghton)
Mari Evans, *I Am A Black Woman* (Morrow)
Lorenz Graham, *Every Man Heart Lay Down* (Crowell)
June Jordan & Terri Bush, *The Voice of the Children* (Holt)
Gloom Grossman, *Black Means* (Hill & Wang)
Margaret W. Peterson, *Ebony Book of Black Achievement* (Johnson Publishing)
Janice May Udry, *Mary Jo's Grandmother* (Whitman)

1970

Lillie Patterson, *Dr. Martin Luther King, Jr., Man of Peace* (Garrard)

ILLUSTRATORS

1990

Jan Spivey Gilchrist, *Nathaniel Talking* by Eloise Greenfield (Black Butterfly)

Honor Books

Jerry Pinkney, *The Talking Eggs* by Robert D. San Souci (Dial)

1989

Jerry Pinkney, *Mirandy and Brother Wind* by Patricia C. McKissack (Knopf)

Honor Books

Amos Ferguson, *Under the Sunday Tree* by Eloise Greenfield (Harper)
Pat Cummings, *Storm in the Night* by Mary Stolz (Harper)

1988

John Steptoe, *Mufaro's Beautiful Daughters* (Lothrop)

Honor Books

Ashley Bryan, *What a Morning! The Christmas Story in Black Spirituals* selected by John Langstaff (Macmillan/ Margaret K, McElderry), Joe Sam, *The Invisible Hunters: A Legend from the Miskito Indians of Nicaragua* compiled by Harriet Rohmer, et al. (Children's Book Press)

1987

Jerry Pinkney, *Half a Moon and One Whole Star* by Crescent Dragonwagon (Macmillan)

Honor Books

Ashley Bryan, *Lion and the Ostrich Chicks and Other African Folk Tales* (Atheneum)
Pat Cummings, *C.L.O.U.D.S.* (Lothrop)

1986

Jerry Pinkney, *The Patchwork Quilt* by Valerie Flournoy (Dial)

Honor Book

Leo & Diane Dillon, *The People Could Fly: American Black Folktales* told by Virginia Hamilton (Knopf)

1984

Pat Cummings, *My Mama Needs Me* by Mildred Pitts Walter (Lothrop)

1983

Peter Magubane, *Black Child* (Knopf)

Honor Books

John Steptoe, *All the Colors of the Race* by Arnold Adoff (Lothrop)
Ashley Bryan, *I'm Going to Sing: Black American Spirituals* (Atheneum)
Pat Cummings, *Just Us Women* by Jeannette Caines (Harper)

1982

John Steptoe, *Mother Crocodile: An Uncle Amadou Tale from Senegal* translated by Rosa Guy (Delacorte)

Honor Book

Tom Feelings, *Daydreamers* by Eloise Greenfield (Dial)

1981

Ashly Bryan, *Beat the Story Drum Pum-Pum* (Atheneum)

Honor Books

Carole Byard, *Grandmama's Joy* Eloise Greenfield (Philomel)
Jerry Pinkney, *Count Off Your Fingers African Style* by Claudia Zaslavsky (Crowell)

1980

Carole Byard, *Cornrows* by Camille Yarbrough (Coward-McCann)

1979

Tom Feelings, *Something on My Mind* by Nikki Grimes (Dial)

1974

George Ford, *Ray Charles* by Sharon Bell Mathis (Crowell)

APPENDIX B

VERBS

The use of English verbs presents a problem for most people who learn it as a second language. Children MUST be taught the principal parts of verbs and how to conjugate them.

To conjugate a verb is to inflect it by giving it various forms, depending upon: (1) tense - present, past, future, present perfect, past perfect, future perfect; (2) number - singular or plural; and (3) person - first person is the one who is speaking, second person is the one spoken to, and third person is the one spoken about.

When children learn verbs, they should be able to use them in their various tenses.

CONJUGATING A VERB
Present Tense

Person	Number	
	Singular	Plural
First (speaking)	I do	we do
Second (spoken to)	You do	you do
Third (spoken about)	he, she, does	they do

* Note: The morpheme -s in English usually means "more than one": boy - boys. However, in English verbs, -s is used to indicate third person singular, present tense: He does his homework. She walks home late at night.

Irregular Verbs

The following list of verbs are considered irregular verbs because they do not use -ed in the past tense. Students must be given numerous opportunities to learn and use these verbs in meaningful contexts. Note that most of these verbs are basic sight vocabulary; they must be recognized instantly just as the basic math facts.

1. Form past participle from present form

Present	Past	Past Participle (with have)
blow	blew	blown
come	came	come
do	did	done
draw	drew	drawn
eat	ate	eaten
fall	fell	fallen
give	gave	given
go	went	gone
ride	rode	ridden
rise	rose	risen
run	ran	run
see	saw	see
shake	shook	shaken
take	took	taken
throw	threw	thrown
write	wrote	written
know	knew	known
grow	grew	grown

2. Same form for all parts

burst
cost
hit
shut
hurt
put
set

3. -en or -n for past form

Present	Past	Past Participle (with have)
beat	beat	beaten
bite	bit	bitten
break	broke	broken
choose	chose	chosen
freeze	froze	frozen
wear	wore	worn

4. Same form for past and past participle

Present	Past	Past Participle
bring	brought	brought
catch	caught	caught
fight	fought	fought
get	got	got
say	said	said

5. Present uses I, past uses A, participle uses U

Present	Past	Past Participle
begin	began	begun
ring	rang	rung
swim	swam	swum
spring	sprang	sprung
drink	drank	drunk
sing	sang	sung
sink	sank	sung

*Note: For an excellent discussion and practice on subject/verb agreement (and many other aspects of English that cause problems) see Milton A. Baxter (1987) *Foundation for Language Learning I and II*. New York: Scribner Education Publishers.

A good way to remember present tense verbs that take -s is: If the subject is plural, the verb does not take an -s ending. But if the subject is third person singular, the verb takes an -s ending.

Present Tense, Third Person

He (third person singular) does his homework on time.
They (third person, singular) do their homework on time.
Studying verbs (the process of studying verbs is third person singular) takes time and effort.
The children (third person plural) study the same time and the same place every day.

Baxter's (1988) *Language Learning I and II* presents an excellent discussion of present tense verbs. Students must be taught to differentiate between singular and plural subjects. Indefinite pronouns frequently cause problems with subject-verb agreement. They do not refer to a definite person or thing; some can be singular, some can be plural and some can be both.

Singular:	Plural:	Singular or Plural:
another	both	all
anybody	few	any
anyone	many	most
anything	several	none
each		some
either		
everybody		
everything		
neither		
nobody		
no one		
one		
somebody		
someone		
something		

Note the following examples:

1. Everyone has the right to learn.
(Everyone is one collective group)
2. Both of the children are here.
(Both means more than one)
3. All of the people were watching the show.
(All refers to every one of the people, so it is plural)
4. All of the cornbread was eaten by him.
(All refers to a single quantity of cornbread, so it must have a singular verb)

See Baxter's materials for a thorough discussion of subject-verb agreement.

Publisher's Note: The publisher uses the words Afrocentricity and Africentricity to show our progress from Afro-American to African American.

REFERENCES

Abrahams, R.D. (1963). Deep down in the jungle. Chicago: Aldine Publishing.

Abrahams, R.D. (1969). Black talk and Black education. The Florida FL Reporter. 3, 10-12.

Abrahams, R.D. (1972). Talking my talk: Black English and social segmentation in Black communities. The Florida FL Reporter. 10 (a), pp. 29-35.

Abrahams, R.D. (1976). Talking Black. Rowley, MA: Newbury House Publishers.

Abrahams, R.D. & G. Gay (1975). Talking Black in the classroom. In P. Stoller (ed.). Black English: Its use in the classroom and in the literature. New York: Dell Publishing, pp. 158-167.

Afrika, L. O. (1990). The Gullah: People blessed by God Revised Gullah Festival Edition, Beaufort, SC: Goldenseal.

Akbar, N. (1990, March 15). Restoration of Black male competence. Paper presented at a conference on male involvement in responsible decision-making, Atlanta, Georgia.

Alexander, C.F. (1985). Black English dialect and the classroom teacher. In C.K. Brooks (ed.), Tapping potential: English and language arts for the Black learner. Urbana, IL., National Council of Teachers of English, pp. 20-29.

Allen, R.V. (1976). Language experiences in communication. Boston: Houghton-Mifflin.

Alleyne, M.C. (1980). Comparative Afro-American, Ann Arbor, MI: Karoma Publishers.

Alvarez, L. & A. Kolker. (1986). American tongues [video-tape]. New Day Films, 853 Broadway, Suite 1210, New York 10003.

Asante, M.K. (1987). The Afrocentric idea. Philadelphia, PA: Temple University Press.

Banks, J.A. (1988). Multiethnic education - Theory and practice. Boston: Allyn and Bacon.

Baugh, J. (1983). Black street speech: Its history, structure, and survival. Austin, TX: University of Texas Press.

Baxter, M. (1986). Foundations for learning I. New York: Scribner Educational Publishers.

Beckford, E.D. (1984). Standard English program handbook. Richmond, California: Richmond Unified School District.

Bernal, M. (1987). Black Athena: The Afrosiatic roots of classical civilization. Vol. I: The fabrication of Ancient Greece. New Brunswick, NJ: Rutgers University Press.

Bickerton, D. (1985). Creole languages. In V.P. Clark, et al.(eds.). Language (4th ed.). New York: St. Martin's Press, pp. 134-151.

Boyer, E. (1983). The high school: A report on secondary education in America. 1st ed., New York: Harper & Row.

Brookover, W. & L. Lezotte (1979). Changes in school characteristics coincident with changes in student achievement, Occasional paper #17. East Lansing, MI: Institute for Research on Teaching.

Brookover, W., et al. (1982). Creating effective schools. Holmes Beach, Fl: Learning Publications.

Brice-Finch, J. (1991, March). George Lamming. 1991 Conference on College Composition and Communication, Boston, Massachusetts.

Burling, R. (1973). English in Black and White. New York: Holt, Rinehart and Winston, Inc.

Chira, S. (1990, August 27-29). Tomorrow's teachers. The New York Times, pp. A1, 1, 13; A1, 12, 13, B8.

Clarke, J.H. (1972). Introduction. In J.A. Rogers (ed.). World's great men of color, Vol. I., Macmillan Pub. Co., pp. ix-xvi.

Cooke, B.G. (1980). No verbal communication among Afro-Americans: An initial classification. In R. Jones (ed.) Black Psychology, 2nd. ed. New York: Harper & Row, pp. 139-160.

Comer, J. (1988). Maggie's American Dream. New York: New American Library.

Cultural diversity classes (1991, January 7). Jet Magazine, p. 10.

Cunningham, P.M. (1976). Teachers' correction responses to Black-dialect miscues which are non-meaning-changing, Reading Research Quarterly. XII(4), pp. 637-653.

Daise, R. (1989). De Gullah storybook. Beaufort, SC: G.O.G. Enterprises.

Dalby, D. (1972). African element in American English. In T. Kochman (ed.) Rappin' and stylin' out, Urbana, IL: University of Illinois Press, pp. 170-186.

Dandy, E.B. (1982). A dialect rejection, Georgia Journal of Reading, (7) p. 22.

Dandy, E.B. (1988). Dialect differences: Do they interfere?. ERIC Document, ED 294-240, 29 pages.

Dandy, E.B. (1990). Consequences of ignoring specific dialect differences. Thresholds in Education (7), pp. 11-15.

Dandy, E.B. (1991, February). Sensitizing teachers to cultural differences: An African American perspective. Resources in Education, ED 323-479, 35 pages.

Davis, O. (1973). The English language is my enemy. In R.H. Bentley (ed.). Black Language Reader, Glenview, IL: Scott Foresman, pp. 71-76.

Delpit, L. (1988, August). The silenced dialogue: Power and pedagogy in educating other people's children, Harvard Educational Review, 58 (3), pp. 280-298.

Dent, D. (1989). Readin', ritin' & rage - How schools are destroying black boys, Essence. 20 (7), pp. 54-56, 59, 116.

Dillard, J.L. (1973). Black English. Its history and usage in the United States. New York: Vintage Books.

Diop, C.A. (1986). African contributions to civilization: The exact sciences. In I. Van Sertima (ed.). Nile Valley Civilizations, Atlanta,GA: Journal of African Civilizations, pp. 69-83.

Diop, C.A. (1986). Origin of the ancient Egyptians. In I. Van Sertima (ed.). Great African Thinkers. New Brunswick, N.J. Transaction Books, pp. 35-63; 167.

Dodson, J. & S. Ross. (1977). Afro-American culture:Expressive behaviors. Atlanta, GA: Atlanta University School of Social Work.

Edmonds, R. (1979). Effective schools for the urban poor, Educational Leadership, 37, pp. 15-24.

Edmonds, R. (1981, October 27). Testimony before the House of Representatives Subcommittee on Elementary, Secondary and Vocational Education. Washington, D.C.

Foster, H.L. (1986). Ribbin', jivin' & playin' the dozens: The persistent dilemma in our schools. 2nd ed., Cambridge, MA: Ballinger Publishing Company.

Gere, A.R. & E. Smith, (1979). Attitudes, language and change. Urbana, IL: National Council of Teachers of English.

Gilliam, D. (1990, November 19). Afrocentric education would benefit all, The Washington Post, section B, pp. 3,4.

Good, T.L. & J.E. Brophy, (1987). Looking in classrooms 4th ed. New York: Harper & Row.

Goodman, K. & C. Buck, (1983, October). Dialect barriers to reading comprehension revisited, The Reading Teacher 27 pp. 6-12.

Greene, A. (1981). Black English in its Proper Perspective. Unpublished paper submitted as requirement of graduate course in English Education, University of South Carolina.

Hale-Benson, J.E. (1986). Black children: Their roots, culture and learning styles, (rev. ed.). Baltimore, MD: Johns Hopkins, 1986.

Hannerz, U. (1977). Growing up male. In D. Wilkerson & R. Taylor (eds.). The Black male in America, Chicago, IL: Nelson Hall, pp. 33-59.

Hare, N. and Hare J. (1987). Bringing the Black boy to manhood. San Francisco, CA: Black Think Tank, p. 16.

Harris, J.B. (1987). African and African-American traditions in language arts. In African American Baseline Essays, Multnomah School District 1J, Portland, OR, pp. LA2-LA23.

Heath, S.B. (1983). Ways with words. Cambridge, MA: Cambridge University Press.

Herskovits, M.J. (1941). The myth of the Negro past, Boston, MA:Beacon Press.

Herskovits, M.J. (1966). The new world Negro. Boston, MA: Minerva Press.

Hill, H.D. (1989). Effective strategies for teaching minority students. Bloomington, Indiana: National Educational Service.

Hilliard, A.G. (1985). Kemetic concepts in education. In I. Van Sertima (ed.)., Nile Valley civilizations, Atlanta, GA: Journal of African Civilization, pp. 153-162.

Holt, G.S. (1972). Stylin outta the Black pulpit. In T. Kochman (ed.). Rappin' and stylin' out. Urbana, IL.: University of Illinois Press, pp. 189-204.

Holy Bible (1969). Authorized King James version. C.I. Scofield (ed.). New York; Oxford University Press, p. 1125.

Hoover, M.R. (1985). Ethnology of Black Communications, Journal of Black Reading/Language Education, 2, pp. 2-4.

Hoover, M.R., N. Dabney and S. Lewis (eds.) (1990). Successful Black and minority schools: Classic models. San Francisco, CA: Julian Richardson Associates.

James, G. G. M. (1954). Stolen legacy. San Francisco, CA: Julian Richardson Associates

Jenifer, F. (1990, November 19). Afrocentricity is no cause for alarm, The Washington Post. Editorial, p. A15.

Johnson, D. and others. (1988). Our cooperative classroom Edina, MN: Interaction Book Company.

Johnson, H.H. (1985). Tips for language teaching: Teacher attitudes and ghetto language. In C.K. Brooks (ed.). Tapping potential: English and language arts for the Black learner. Urbana, IL: Black Caucus of the National Council of Teachers of English, pp. 75, 77.

Johnson, J. (1980, March 15). The endangered Black male: The new bald eagle. Paper presented at a Conference on Male Involvement in Responsible Decision-Making, Atlanta, Georgia.

Johnson, K. (1972). The vocabulary of race. In T. Kochman (ed.). Rappin' and stylin' out, Urbana, IL: University of Illinois Press, pp. 140-151.

Johnson, K. (1975, April). Black dialect shift in oral reading, The Reading Teacher, 28, pp. 535-540.

Kochman, T. (1981). Black and White styles in conflict. Chicago, IL: University of Chicago Press.

Kunjufu, J. (1986). Countering the conspiracy to destroy Black boys, Vol. I and II, Chicago, IL: African American Images.

Kunjufu, J. (1987). Lessons from history - a celebration in blackness - elementary or high school edition. Chicago, IL: African American Images.

Kunjufu, J. (1988). To be popular or smart: The Black peer group. Chicago, IL: African American Images.

Labov. W. (1970). The study of nonstandard English. Champaign, IL: National Council of Teachers of English.

Larned, G. (1990, February 21). Economic development and well-being in the Black community. Paper presented at panel discussion sponsored by Health Professions Career Opportunity Program, Armstrong State College.

Leonard, C.M. and M.B. Aradar (1988). (Eds.). African-American lesson plans grades K-5. Portland, OR: Multicultural/Multiethnic Education Office.

Levine, L.W. (1977). Freedom, culture and religion. In L.W. Levin (ed.). Black culture and Black consciousness. New York:Oxford University Press.

Lumpkin, B. (1983). Mathematics and engineering in the Nile Valley. In I. Van Sertima (ed.). Nile Valley Civilizations, Atlanta, GA: Journal of African Civilizations, pp. 100-109.

Madden, J.V., D.R. Lawsen & D. Sweet (1976). Schools effectiveness study: State of South Carolina. Paper presented at the annual meeting of American Educational Research Association, San Francisco, CA.

Maxwell, J. (1974). On learning a second dialect: A position paper. Dialects and Learning, Urbana, IL: National Council of Teachers of English.

Mays, L. (1980). The use of street games in language programs.In J.I. Schwartz (ed.).Teaching the linguistically diverse. New York: New York State English Council, pp. 76-89.

Mbiti, J. (1990). African religions and philosophy, 2nd ed. Portsmouth, NH: Heinemann Educational Books.

Mille, K. (1990). A historical analysis of tense - mood - aspect in Gullah creole: A case of stable variation. Doctoral dissertation, University of South Carolina.

Miller, P. (1986). Nonverbal Communication, 2nd. ed. Washington, DC: National Education Association.

Mitchell-Kernan, C. (1972). Signifying, loud-talking and marking. In T. Kochman (ed.). Rappin' and stylin' out: Communication in urban Black America. Urbana, IL: University of Illinois Press, pp. 315-335.

Mussen, P.H., J.J. Conger and J. Kagan (1956). Child development and personality 4th ed., New York: Harper & Row, Publishers.

Nelson-Barber, S. & T. Meier (1990). Multicultural context a key factor in teaching. Academic Connections. New York:Office of Academic Affairs, the College Board, pp. 1-5, 9-11.

Nichols, P.C. (1989, November). Language in the attic: Claiming our linguistic heritage. Paper presented at the National Council of Teachers of English panel on Diversity as a Resource: Redefining Cultural Literacy, Baltimore, MD.

Nichols, P.C. (1989). Storytelling in Carolina: Continuities and contrasts. Anthropology and Education Quarterly, 20 (3), pp. 232-245.

Nobles, W.W. (1980). African philosophy: Foundation for Black psychology. In R.J. Jones (Ed.). Black Psychology, 2nd ed., New York: Harper & Row, pp. 23-36.

Pearson, B.L. (1977). Introduction to linguistic concepts, New York: Alfred A. Knopf.

Phi Delta Kappan (1980). Why do some urban schools succeed? Bloomington, Indiana.

Pike, P. (1987). Wordbuster reading rap, Chicago, IL: Pike Unlimited.

Pine, G.J. & A.G. Hilliard (1990, April). Rx for racism: Imperatives for America's schools. Phi Delta Kappan. pp.593-600.

Roots (1977). Warner Home Video, Volumes I-VI, Burbank, CA: Wolper Pictures, 4000 Warner Blvd.

Ross, E. & B. Roe (1990). An introduction to the teaching of language arts. New York: Holt, Rinehart & Winston.

Schultz, D.A. (1977). Coming up as a boy in the ghetto. In D. Wilkinson and R. Taylor (eds.). The Black male in America, Chicago, Nelson Hall, pp. 7-32.

Scott, J.C. (1985). Language and the teaching-learning process. In C.K. Brooks (ed.), Tapping potential: English and language arts for the Black learner. Urbana, IL: National Council of Teachers of English, pp. 9-11.

Scotton, C.M. (1978). Codeswitching as a "safe choice" in choosing lingua franca. In McCormack and S. Wurm (eds). Language and Society, The Hague: Mouton Publishers.

Sheppard, V. (1990, Summer). August Wilson: An interview. National Forum, pp. 7-11.

Shuy, R. (1975). Teacher training an urban language problem. In P. Stoller (ed.) Black American English: Its background and its usage in

schools and in literature. New York: Dell
Publishing, pp. 168-185.

Shuy, R. (1985). Dialects: How they differ. In V.P.
Clark, P.A. Eschholz, A.F. Rosa (eds.) Language
introductory readings. New York: St. Martin's
Press, pp. 500-512.

Sims, R. (1972). A psycholingustic description of
miscues generated by selected young readers
during the oral reading of text material in Black
dialect and standard English. Doctoral
dissertation, Wayne State University, Detroit, MI

Sithole, E.T. (1972). Black folk music. In T.
Kochman (ed.).Rappin' and stylin' out, Urbana, IL:
University of Illinois Press, pp. 65-82.

Slavin, R.E. (1987). Cooperative learning: Student
teams (2nd ed.). Washington, DC: National
Education Assoc.

Sledd, J. (1965). On not teaching English usage.
English Journal, LIV, p. 702.

Smith, E.A. (1974). The evaluation and continuing
presence of the African oral tradition in Black
America. Doctoral dissertation, University of
California, Irvine.

Smitherman, G. (1977). Talkin and testifyin',
Boston: Houghton Mifflin Company.

Stice, C.F. (1987 Fall/Winter). Making dialect
differences work for children. Georgia Journal of
Reading, pp. 15-20.

Stoller, P. (1975). The case against Black English in
the schools: A brief review. In P. Stoller (ed.),
Black American English. New York: Dell
Publishing Company, pp. 4-6.

Stover, D. (1990, June). In new racism, The American School Board Journal. pp. 14-18.

Strickland, D. (1985). Early Childhood development and reading instruction. In C.K. Brooks (ed.). Tapping potential: English and language arts for the Black learner. Urbana, IL: National Council of Teachers of English, pp. 88-101.

Sy, J. H. (1989). Theophile Obenga: At the forefront of Egypto-Nubian and Black African renaissance in philosophy. In I. Van Sertima (ed.). Egypt revisited, 2nd ed., New Brunswick, U.S.A.: Journal of African Civilizations, Ltd., pp. 277-285.

Tarynor, N.K. (1976). The impact of the African tradition on African christianity .Ann Arbor, MI: Xerox University Microfilms, self-published edition.

Taylor, O. (1986). A cultural and communicative approach to teaching standard English as a second dialect. In O. Taylor (ed.). Treatment of communication disorders in culturally and linguistically diverse populations. San Diego, CA: College-Hill Press, pp. 153-178.

Taylor, O. (1987). Cross-cultural communication - An essential dimension of effective education. Washington, DC: Mid- Atlantic Center for Race Equity.

Taylor, O. (1990). Cross-cultural communication - An essential dimension of effective education. 2nd. ed., Washington, DC: Mid-Atlantic Center for Race Equity.

Thompson, R.F. (1981). Flash of the spirit: African and Afro-American art and philosophy. New York: Random House.

Townsend, A.M. (ed). (1973). The baptist standard hymnal. Nashville, TN: Sunday School Publishing Board.

Turner, L.D. (1949). Africanisms in the Gullah dialect. Ann Arbor, MI: University of Michigan Press.

Turner, D.T. (1985). Black students, language, and classroom teachers. In C.K. Brooks (ed.). Tapping potential: English and language arts for the Black learner. Urbana, IL: Black Caucus of the National Council Teachers of English, pp. 30-40.

Van Sertima, I. (1971). African linguistic and mythological structures in the new world. In R.L. Goldstein (ed.). Black life and culture in the United States. New York: Thomas Y. Crowell, pp. 12-35.

Van Sertima, I. (1976). My Gullah brother and I: Exploration into a community's language and myth through its oral tradition. In D.S. Harrison and T. Trabasso (eds.). Black English: a seminar. Hillsdale, N.J.: Lawrence Erlbaum, pp. 123-146.

Van Sertima, I. (1985). Nile Valley civilizations. In I. Van Sertima (ed.). Journal of African Civilization. New Brunswick, NJ, pp. 16-21.

Van Sertima, I. (1989). Blacks in science: Ancient and modern. New Brunswick, NJ: Journal of African Civilizations, Ltd.

Vass, W.K. (1979). Bantu speaking heritage of the United States Los Angeles, CA: Center for Afro-American Studies, University of California.

Walker, W.T. (1987). Spirits that dwell in deep woods. New York: Martin Luther King Fellows Press.

Warfield-Coppack, N. (1990). Afrocentric theory and applications, Vol. I: Adolescent Rites of Passage.Washington, DC: Boabab Associates.

Watkins, E., Terrill, F. and others (1989). Cultural mistrust and its effects on expectation variables in

Black - client White counselor relationship. _Journal of Counseling Psychology_, 36 (4), pp. 447-450.

Weber, G. (1971). _Inner city children can be taught to read:Four successful schools_. Washington, DC: Council for Basic Education.

Welmers, W.E. (1973). _African language structures_. Berkley, CA: University of California Press.

Wolfram, W. and R. Fasold (1974). _The study of social dialects in American English_, Englewood Cliffs, N.J.: Prentice-Hall,Inc.

Woods, K. (1983, October). Four-way reading. _The Reading Teacher_. 36 (1) pp. 38-41.

Woodson, G.C. (1933). _The miseducation of the Negro_. Philadelphia, PA: Hamkim's Publication.

Ya' ari, E. & I. Friedman. (1991, February). Curses in verses. _The Atlantic_, 267 (2), pp. 22-26.

Yellin, D. (1980). The Black English Controversy: Implications from the Ann Arbor Case. _Journal of Reading_ 24, pp. 150-154.

Footnotes

ch1-1
For a legal application to this concept see
  Smitherman's and Scott's discussion of Martin
  Luther King Junior Elementary School Children v.
  Ann Arbor School District Board in *Tapping
  Potential,* pp. 41-62; 63-71.

ch4-1
Baxter (1966) Foundations for Learning Language 1.
  New York: Scribner Educational Publishers pp.
  88-89. This is an excellent series designed for
  middle and high school development.

ch4-2
From "Vocabulary List of Possible Bantu Origin",
  Vass (1979) Bantu Speaking Heritage of the United
  States, pp. 105-122 and "Some aspects of English
  in Liberia;" Hancock (1975) Perspective on Black
  English, pp.248-25.